MORE
Words
You
Should
Know

MORE
Words You Should Know

Michelle Bevilacqua

ADAMS MEDIA CORPORATION
Holbrook, Massachusetts

Published by
Adams Media Corporation
260 Center Street, Holbrook, MA 02343

ISBN: 1-55850-293-9

Printed in the United States of America

D   E   F   G   H   I   J

Library of Congress Cataloging-in-Publication Data
Bevilacqua, Michelle.
    More words you should know : more words every educated person
should be able to use and define / Michelle Bevilacqua.
    p.   cm.
    ISBN 1-55850-293-9
    1. Vocabulary.
    PE1449.B47   1994
    423'.1—dc20   93-47470
                                                            CIP

*This book is available at quantity discounts for bulk purchases.
For information, call 1-800-872-5627
(in Massachusetts, 617-767-8100).*

Visit our home page at http://www.adamsmedia.com

Acknowledgments

Thank you, thank you, thank you to everyone who offered their support, ideas, words, and sentences. Special thanks to Erica Jorgensen for always having something to offer, to Kate Layzer for her usual superlative copyediting job, and to Brandon Toropov for pitching in in the final weeks. I would also like to extend my gratitude to Dawn Costello for her many invaluable contributions. Finally, I would like to acknowledge all of the wonderful teachers and professors I've had over the years who have not only enhanced my vocabulary, but also instilled in me a love of language and knowledge.

Introduction

One of the main advantages of this book is what it does not contain. Reading the dictionary is virtually no one's idea of a thrilling time. Accordingly, this book has been designed to be that rarity among reference and vocabulary books: one you can leaf through enjoyably. You will not find here long chunks of dense type examining the thirty-one different potential uses of the word *make*. The focus here is on the most popularly employed senses of tough-but-common words. Where a word is in common usage in more than one main sense—as both a noun and a verb, for instance—both of the common definitions are included. No attempt is made here to render every conceivable usage of every word included in this book. That would be boring. The objective of *More Words You Should Know*, as of its predecessor, is simply to help you become familiar with the most common senses of the troublesome words you are likely to encounter.

A side note: this book features U.S. state names and capitals as well, as these too are the source of frequent problems; look under the name of the state to find the name of the capital in question.

More Words You Should Know

abacus (AB-uh-kuss): a device used to figure arithmetic equations by moving beads along rods.

> *Mrs. Danvers thought that the ABACUS, with its brightly colored beads, would entertain the first graders while illustrating the basic principles of addition and subtraction.*

abase (uh-BASE): to humiliate or deprive of self-worth.

> *Melanie refused to ABASE herself for her boss over a simple clerical error.*

abbess (AB-iss): a head nun in charge of a convent; a mother superior.

> *The old ABBESS generally ran a strict convent, so on my birthday I was amazed to find she'd left a box of chocolates on my reading table.*

abbreviated (uh-BREE-vee-ate-ud): shortened.

> *Because the hour is late, I will limit myself to an ABBREVIATED version of my intended speech.*

abduct (ub-DUCT): to take a person away secretly and illegally, often by use of force; to kidnap.

> *My sister Ellen used to take such long showers that Dad would jokingly ask if she'd been ABDUCTED by aliens.*

aberrant (AB-uh-runt): abandoning the correct, expected, or proper way of doing things; straying from the "right" or norm.

> *Alice's decision to quit college and tour the country on motorcycle seemed so ABERRANT to her parents that they asked her to get a psychiatric evaluation.*

abeyance (uh-BEY-unce): temporary suspension; a temporary pause, especially in regard to a government or court's ruling.

> *To the embarrassment of the school administration, the local newspaper soon got wind of their decision to hold Chuck's expulsion in ABEYANCE and allow him to play in the championship game.*

abominate (uh-BOM-ih-nate): to loathe or hate; to view with extreme hostility.

> *Miss Green ABOMINATED the notion of children working twelve-hour days, and sought legislation forbidding companies from hiring minor workers.*

absinthe (AB-sinth): A green alcoholic liqueur flavored with wormwood and having narcotic qualities.

> *Before the beverage was banned in the early part of this century, a great many Americans were addicted to ABSINTHE.*

absolution (ab-suh-LOO-shun): the condition of having been forgiven or freed of guilt.

> *To Myron's dismay, the judge did not consider his having paid for the damage to the other party's car sufficient ABSOLUTION for the crime of driving while intoxicated.*

abstain (ub-STANE): to refrain from; to refuse to partake in; to go without voluntarily.

Maria, who had ABSTAINED from eating meat while in high school, was persuaded to try a cheeseburger on her graduation night.

abyss (uh-BISS): an endless black void; an emptiness; a huge hole with no bottom.

After nine days of working on my term paper with no conclusion in sight, I felt more and more as if I were facing an ABYSS.

accept (ak-SEPT): to take into possession. (See, for comparison, the listing for *except*.)

I'm happy to ACCEPT your invitation to dinner, Claude.

acclimated (AK-lih-may-tud): having-adapted or become accustomed to.

At first Tami found college life lonely and stressful, but after a few weeks she became ACCLIMATED and never longed for home again.

accost (uh-KOST): to greet or approach, usually in a confrontational way; to approach in order to confront.

I was having a wonderful time at Sara's wedding until Uncle George ACCOSTED me at the bar and demanded to know when I planned to get a real job.

acme (AK-me): the highest point; summit.

Although his many fans might consider winning the Pulitzer the ACME of Marvin's writing career, in his mind nothing would ever match the thrill of seeing his first novel in print.

acronym (AK-ruh-nim): a word formed by combining the first letters of several other words. (Example: NOW is an acronym for the National Organization for Women.)

> *Cindy believed that the secret to getting good grades on tests was to use ACRONYMS as memory aids.*

acuity (uh-KUE-uh-tee): keen, as in the mind or the senses; deft.

> *Although Professor Kane admitted that Jordan's chess ACUITY was impressive for one so young, he did not agree that the boy was ready to compete professionally.*

adapt (uh-DAPT): to adjust; to make something or oneself fit in to particular circumstances; to conform. (See, for comparison, the entry for *adopt*.)

> *Jim and Daisy worried that the cross-country move would upset their teenage daughter, but as it turned out Melanie ADAPTED to their new home more easily than her parents.*

adhere (ad-HERE): to hold fast to, usually with a sense of honor or allegiance.

> *Even after his career in advertising forced him to move to New York City, Mason continued to ADHERE to the values of his strict Mormon upbringing.*

adjunct (AD-junkt): an unessential addition; an appendage or complement.

> *Fast cars and designer clothes are only ADJUNCTS to a comfortable lifestyle, Lyle argued, while health insurance is something a family simply can't do without.*

12

ad lib (ad lib): an off the cuff, spontaneous remark; also, to make such a remark.

I marveled at Erika's ability to AD LIB her way through the meeting, knowing as I did that she hadn't even read the annual report.

adobe (uh-DOE-bee): a type of brick made of clay and straw; the clay used to form such bricks.

Our anthropology professor informed us that ADOBE huts are viable only in climates with very little rainfall.

adopt (uh-DOPT): to accept or take as one's own. (See, for comparison, the entry for *adapt*.)

After last year's car troubles, I've ADOPTED the philosophy that a good mechanic is worth every penny you pay him.

adrenaline (uh-DREN-uh-lin): a chemical produced in the body that gives one added strength and energy; epinephrine.

Having run up and down the basketball court for nearly and hour, Bob hoped for a burst of ADRENALINE to carry him through to the end of the game.

adverse (AD-verse): unfavorable; acting in opposition to. Also: tending to discourage. (See, for comparison, the entry for *averse*).

Despite ADVERSE circumstances, Jenny and I managed, after a month of looking, to find an apartment we could afford.

affable (AFF-uh-bul): gentle; approachable; friendly.

We were all sad to see our old boss leave, but relieved that his replacement seemed like an AFFABLE person.

affect (uh-FEKT): to influence; to stir the emotions of; to produce an effect (in something). (See, for comparison, the entry for *effect*.)

> *The memory of my parents' hideous and protracted breakup AFFECTED my life profoundly, and made me vow to work harder at making my own marriage succeed.*

agrarian (uh-GRARE-ee-un): relating to or concerning the land or farming.

> *It amazed the census taker that these farmers, living only a short drive from the big city, could maintain their small AGRARIAN community with so little difficulty.*

ague (AG-you): a malarial fever marked by drastic fits of hot and cold sweats.

> *Our expedition down the Nile came to an abrupt halt when our navigator was struck with an attack of AGUE.*

aid (aid): to help. (See, for comparison, the entry for *aide*.)

> *Please help our organizations efforts to AID these refugees.*

aide (aide): an assistant. (See, for comparison, the entry for *aid*.)

> *Wilson, my AIDE, will see that you get the materials you need.*

Alabama (al-uh-BAM-uh): the twenty-second state of the United States.

> *The capital of ALABAMA is Montgomery.*

Alaska (uh-LASS-kuh): the forty-ninth state of the United States.

> *The capital of ALASKA is Juneau.*

alchemy (AL-kuh-mee): a medieval chemical philosophy in which the goal was to convert base metals into gold; also, any supposedly magical power of transformation or instant creation of wealth.

Staring at a printout indicating an 83-percent shortfall in projected income for the first three quarters, the president of the firm remarked bitterly that an ALCHEMY department would do the firm more good than its research and development team had.

alibi (AL-uh-bye): a story or circumstance that proves one is innocent of a crime or misdeed; a credible excuse or explanation of innocence.

Mike promised Craig he'd provide him with an ALIBI for the night of the bank robbery, but when the police questioned the men they found that the details of their stories didn't match.

allegiance (uh-LEE-junce): loyalty, particularly to a government.

Alex had promised his ALLEGIANCE to the family firm time and time again, but the new offer from their overseas competitor, he decided, was too good to turn down.

allegory (AL-uh-gore-ee): a story that seems simple on the surface but that uses symbolism and other techniques to convey a deeper meaning, usually one relevant to major ethical or social issues.

Dr. Seuss's Yertle the Turtle, *a delightful children's story, is also an ALLEGORY about the dangers of fascism and megalomania.*

alleviate (uh-LEEV-ee-ate): to make more bearable; to relieve.

The only thing that will ALLEVIATE the fatigue I'm feeling right now is a good night's sleep.

alliterative (uh-LIT-er-ah-tive): using the repetition of initial consonant sounds in language.

"Peter Piper picked a peck of pickled peppers" is an ALLITERATIVE tongue-twister.

alluring (uh-LOOR-ing): tempting; possessing the power to entice.

Although Kim was following a strict diet, the chocolates were too ALLURING for her to resist.

ally (AL-lie): a confederate or fellow associate in a cause. Also, as a verb: to join with another in a common pursuit.

With Jones as my ALLY, I knew the project was more likely to be approved.

aloof (uh-LOOF): indifferent or uninterested; unsociable.

Chuck's ALOOF attitude at our dinner party made us wonder if our usually talkative friend was trying to tell us something.

already (all-RED-ee): at a past time. (Note that this is a single word, and should not be confused with "all ready," meaning completely prepared.)

I ALREADY looked up those figures you need, Mr. Smith.

altar (ALL-tur): a platform in a church or synagogue. (See, for comparison, the entry for *alter*.)

> *Father Miller stood and addressed us from the ALTAR.*

alter (ALL-tur): to cause to change. (See, for comparison, the entry for *altar*.)

> *I could tell that the documents had been ALTERED; they featured two different sets of handwriting in two shades of ink.*

ambiguous (am-BIG-yoo-uss): unclear in meaning; open to more than one interpretation. (See, for comparison, the entry on *ambivalent*.)

> *The letter from my mother was AMBIGUOUS as to the date of the family reunion, so we will have to call her to get the specifics.*

ambivalent (am-BIV-uh-lunt): uncertain or undecided. (See, for comparison, the entry on *ambiguous*.)

> *I'm AMBIVALENT as to whether we should invite Ralph to the party; he's a great storyteller, but he sometimes drinks too much.*

amend (uh-MEND); to modify or update. (See, for comparison, the entry on *emend*.)

> *In light of the testimony we've heard tonight, Madame President, I'd like to AMEND my earlier remarks.*

ampersand (AM-per-sand): the symbol "&"; represents the word "and."

> *For the corporate logo she was designing, the graphic artist decided to use an AMPERSAND instead of the bulkier word "and."*

andante (on-DONT-ay): moderately slow tempo.

"Goodness, Sarah," exclaimed the music teacher, "it says 'ANDANTE,' but you don't have to play it like a dirge!"

androgynous (an-DROJ-ih-nuss): neither specifically male nor female; appearing with both male and female characteristics.

Amy said her new short haircut was a breeze to maintain compared to the long mane she used to have, but I thought it made her look rather ANDROGYNOUS.

anemic (uh-NEE-mik): of or pertaining to a medical condition in which one's blood is deficient in red corpuscles; also, extraordinarily weak.

I made a few ANEMIC efforts to get some work done last night, but I couldn't really focus on the job at hand.

anomie (an-uh-MEE): in society, unrest or instability that arises from a collapse in values and systems of order; for an individual, feelings of alienation, insecurity, and discontent, largely do to one's loss or confusion over ideals or purpose in life.

There were some who speculated that the dismal state of the economy, combined with a general feeling of ANOMIE among citizens, could lead the country to revolution.

anorexia nervosa (an-uh-rex-ee-uh nur-VOH-suh): a disease in which the sufferer has a morbid fear of being obese and loses weight by means of virtual starvation, refusing to stop even when nearly emaciated.

The late Karen Carpenter's was perhaps the most widely publicized case of ANOREXIA NERVOSA.

anthropomorphic (an-thro-puh-MORE-fik):
Attributing human characteristics to animals or other
nonhumans.

> *Walt Disney knew that his ANTHROPOMORPHIC
> creations would be important to the success of his films.*

anticlimactic (an-tee-klie-MAK-tik): a disappointing
decline in contrast to a previous rise; an average ending to a
series of important events.

> *Mike got down on his knees and produced a small velvet
> box, only to reveal a tiny pewter thimble bearing a replica
> of the Golden Gate Bridge—which Elizabeth found
> ANTICLIMACTIC, to say the least.*

antonym (AN-tuh-nim): a word having an opposite
meaning to that of another word.

> *"Rapid" and "slow" are ANTONYMS.*

apéritif (uh-pair-uh-teef): An alcoholic beverage
consumed before a meal.

> *The clock struck six o'clock and the guests at the dinner
> party were served APERITIFS.*

apex (AY-pex): the highest point.

> *The APEX of Dawn's career came when her novel was
> made into a miniseries starring Elizabeth Taylor as the
> heroine.*

aphasia (uh-FAY-zhuh): the inability, brought on by brain
damage, to understand words and/or ideas.

> *After his car accident Marcus retained all of his physical
> faculties, but suffered minor APHASIA that made it
> difficult for him to speak coherently.*

apparel (uh-PAIR-ul): clothing; something worn.

After sweating through class after class in the heavy wool uniform, I wanted to march to the principal's office and demand to know why shorts were considered inappropriate APPAREL for school.

appease (uh-PEEZE): to placate; to soothe or satisfy.

I only wore the dress to APPEASE my mother, who had made pointed comments all week about people who went to weddings dressed like slobs.

appraise (uh-PRAZE): to estimate (an item's) value. (See, for comparison, the entry for *apprise*.)

This desk has been in our family for over a hundred years and I wouldn't dream of selling it—so there's really no use in getting it APPRAISED, is there?

apprentice (uh-PREN-tiss): one who is learning a trade or art form by assisting a veteran practitioner or professional.

Uncle Jake offered to let me work as an APPRENTICE in his plumbing business for the summer, but I had no interest in water pipes.

apprise (uh-PRIZE): to notify; to cause to be aware of. (See, for comparison, the entry for *appraise*.)

Have you been APPRISED of the most recent news from home?

archaic (ar-KAY-ik): relating to or resembling something from the past; antiquated.

Grandma refused to use our washing machine to clean clothes, insisting instead on her ARCHAIC washboard and bucket.

archival (are-KIE-vul): of or pertaining to important records or archives.

After the lab fire, the scientist was less disturbed by the loss of equipment and samples than by the destruction of the contents of his ARCHIVAL vault, a loss that set his work back at least six months.

ardor (AR-dur): intense passion, desire, or emotion.

Since childhood, Michelle had studied animals with such ARDOR that her friends and family encouraged her to become a veterinarian.

Arizona (air-ih-ZONE-uh): the forty-eighth state of the United States.

The capital of ARIZONA is Phoenix.

Arkansas (AR-kun-saw): the twenty-fifth state of the United States.

The capital of ARKANSAS is Little Rock.

arson (AR-con): the act of destroying property with fire.

After Councilor Perry's campaign headquarters burned down, his supporters were quick to accuse their opponents of ARSON; in fact, one of their own neglected cigarette butts was to blame.

ascend (uh-SEND): to go up; to rise or move upward.

As the new attorney quickly ASCENDED within the ranks of the law firm, he couldn't help noticing that his coworkers appeared less than happy for him.

ascertain (ass-sur-TANE): to find out something by experimenting or by making inquiries.

> *Arriving to find the house locked and shuttered, I ASCERTAINED from the neighbors that my fiance had loaded up a moving van and fled the day before.*

aspiration (ass-puh-RAY-shun): goal; desire; something one wishes to achieve.

> *Marco, whose ASPIRATION was to be a concert violinist, practiced his instrument at least eight hours a day.*

assay (UH-say): to test or examine; to check out.

> *My insurance company would not settle my accident claim until an adjuster had ASSAYED the damage to the car.*

assent (uh-SENT): to agree that an opinion, view, or proposal is correct; to concur, corroborate, or acquiesce.

> *You forget, Mr. Jameson, that it is only with the ASSENT of the stockholders that the CEO can be ousted.*

assuage (uh-SWAJE): to ease; to make less severe; to mitigate.

> *Gary tried to ASSUAGE his grief at the loss of his lover by taking a long trip to Europe.*

astute (uh-STUTE): skilled; quick to learn or grasp; shrewd; sharp-witted.

> *Carl was an ASTUTE investor who knew when to follow the crowd and when to ignore it.*

asunder (uh-SUN-dur): into pieces or parts; separated.

The lightning bolt had torn the old hickory tree ASUNDER, and it now lay shattered and twisted in my grandparents' yard.

atavistic (at-uh-VIS-tic): having characteristics regressing to a more primitive type; resembling a distant relative.

I can't help thinking that when the men all congregate around the barbecue, some ATAVISTIC instinct from the stone age is at work.

attenuate: to spread thin; to cause a decrease in amount, value, power, severity.

Jim's strategy was to ATTENUATE the impact of Joan's accusations of harassment by suggesting that she had somehow invited his overtures.

au contraire (oh kon-TRARE): on the contrary; the opposite.

"AU CONTRAIRE, you pompous fool, " cried Jeanne; "I'm not playing hard to get at all, but rather despise you with all my heart!"

au courant (oh kuh-RONT): up-to-date; current.

Mary Ann prided herself on her ability to stay AU COURANT with the latest trends in fashion.

auger (AW-gur): a tool for drilling holes. (See, for comparison, the entry for *augur*.)

I couldn't use my father's drill because the AUGER was missing.

augur (AW-gur): to foretell future events, as though by supernatural knowledge or power; to divine; to indicate a future trend or happening. (See, for comparison, the entry for *auger*.)

> *The chairman's sour mood this morning does not AUGUR well for that budget proposal we made.*

au naturel (oh nat-choo-RELL): as is, without embellishment or adornment; also, nude.

> *Karen wanted to crawl under the table when her mother started showing her fiance the family photo album, which featured a number of embarrassing photo of her on the changing table, AU NATUREL.*

au revoir (oh rih-VWAHR): goodbye; until we meet again.

> *I thought I had bid my last party guest "AU REVOIR," and was about to retire for the night, when I found Philbert passed out in the bathtub.*

augment (og-MENT): to make bigger; increase; enhance.

> *The evening's program—a series of soliloquies from Shakespeare—was AUGMENTED by a short reading from Bradley's* Notes on Hamlet.

autism (AW-tiz-um): a condition in which the sufferer has difficulty with or indifference to social contact, residing almost exclusively in his or her own world.

> *Often subjected to abuse and inhumane treatment two or three decades ago, those suffering from AUTISM are now more likely to receive a meaningful therapeutic regimen.*

autonomous (aw-TAHN-uh-muss): being in charge of one's own life; independent of other influences; self-governing.

Peter had always struggled to remain AUTONOMOUS after leaving home, so it was no surprise to us that he chose to start his own business after graduation.

auxiliary (auk-ZIL-yuh-ree): backup, reserve, extra.

"Don't panic," Mr. Forrest told his anxious staff after the office went black; "the AUXILIARY power will come on any minute now, and we'll be back in business."

averse (uh-VERCE): holding a disinclination. (See, for comparison, the entry for *adverse*.)

I'm afraid the problem is not that Tom can't find a field of study he enjoys; it's that he's AVERSE to the idea of doing any work.

aversion (uh-VUR-zhun): extreme dislike; loathing.

My AVERSION to soap operas leaves me with little to discuss at coffee breaks.

avid (A-vid): earnest; eager; passionate and committed.

Ralphie, an AVID Pittsburgh Steelers fan, owned posters, pennants, hats, socks, jackets, shirts, sweatshirts, and underwear bearing his team's logo and colors, but his wife had drawn the line at a tattoo.

avoid (uh-VOID): to shun; to stay removed from. (See, for comparison, the entry for *evade*.)

At all costs, AVOID the Chef's Surprise at Trudy's Whistlestop Cafe.

azimuth (AZ-uh-muth): the distance in degrees in a clockwise direction from the southernmost point of a body.

The AZIMUTH between the main mast and the sea varied as the boat pitched in the waves.

azure (AZH-uhr): the color of the sky on a clear day; sky-blue.

His AZURE eyes and charming manner may attract women initially, but his conceited personality keeps them from staying interested for long.

bacchanalian (back-uh-NAIL-yuhn): drunken and carousing.

The fraternity brothers seemed to have an insatiable appetite for BACCHANALIAN revelry.

baleful (BAIL-ful): ominous; signaling evil to come.

It always seemed to me that Mrs. Howard had a BALEFUL gleam in her eye as she passed out her absurdly difficult tests.

ballistics (buh-LISS-tiks): the study of projectiles and impacts.

Each of the scientists working on the missile project had extensive experience in BALLISTICS.

balk (bock): to hesitate and refuse to go forward; to prevent from accomplishing an aim; to stop oneself in order to consider whether or not to go on. In baseball: to perform an illegal maneuver in the delivery of a throw from the pitching mound; an instance of such an illegal delivery.

At first Mona BALKED at the suggestion that she apply for the position in management; she did not like the idea of working late hours.

bamboozle (bam-BOO-zul): to deceive; trick.

Fred was BAMBOOZLED out of $15,000 by a con artist, who convinced him to invest money in nonexistent real estate.

banal (buh-NAHL): trite; unoriginal.

Aaron always dismissed the insights of the other philosophers as BANAL, but I for one never heard him utter a single profound idea.

baritone (BARE-uh-tone): the second-deepest voice range on the scale, higher than bass and deeper than treble.

Given his diminutive stature and shy demeanor, few suspected that Craig's powerful BARITONE would dominate the choir.

barometer (buh-ROM-uh-ter): an instrument that measures air pressure and aids in weather prediction.

After a lesson on meteorology, Mr. Cantelli put a BAROMETER up on the classroom's outer wall so that his students could practice predicting the weather.

basilica (buh-SILL-ih-kuh): an oblong building used as a Christian church, especially one built in medieval Italy with strong horizontal accents and little attempt at rhythmic internal design; a building reminiscent of such a structure.

The highlight of our visit to Rome was our visit to St. Peter's BASILICA.

bathos (BATH-oss): something excessively trivial, sentimental, or melodramatic; also, a ludicrous change from the high-minded to the commonplace.

The play's BATHOS made it hard for me to take it seriously, but June thought it was the most moving drama she had ever seen.

bazaar (buh-ZAR): a marketplace, especially one in the open air. (See, for comparison, the entry for *bizarre.*)

> *As Ned and I ambled through the BAZAARS of Casablanca, we kept an eye out for enemy agents.*

bedlam (BED-lum): a state of agitation, furor, or confusion.

> *Even elite squads of riot police could not control the BEDLAM that erupted in the city after the trial's verdict was announced.*

benchmark (BENCH-mark): a standard by which to measure; the exemplary performance or criterion.

> *Anne's stunning oration on human rights was recognized in our debating society as the BENCHMARK performance for years afterward.*

besiege (bih-SEEJ): to submit a person or body to insistent demands from all sides; to crowd around; to harass.

> *Everywhere he went, the movie idol was BESIEGED by crazed fans looking for autographs and even pieces of his hair or clothing.*

betrothed (bih-TROTHED): engaged to be married. Also, as a noun: the person to whom one is engaged.

> *Marcia is BETROTHED to that handsome young captain she met in Miami.*

biased (BYE-ussed): predisposed to a particular view or direction; prejudiced.

> *Mr. Anderson's claim that he has never made a BIASED hiring decision is undercut by the fact that his staff is composed exclusively of white male Ivy League graduates.*

bibelot (BEE-buh-low): a beautiful trinket.

> *The rest of the family dismissed the contents of Grandma's jewelry box as junk, but I found a few BIBELOTS.*

biennial (bye-EN-ee-yul): happening every second year.

> *Ms. Webster argues that the summer Olympics, which now occur every four years, should become a BIENNIAL event.*

bilge (bilj): the lowest portion of a ship's hull.

> *The sailors ventured down to the bowels of the ship to find that the BILGE had sprung a leak.*

billet-doux (bill-ay-DOO): a love letter. (Plural: billets-doux.)

> *The young couple exchanged BILLETS-DOUX almost every day the summer they were apart.*

biopsy (BIE-op-see): an instance of taking samples of tissue, cells, or fluids from a living body and analyzing these samples.

> *Dr. Smith thought the lump was probably a benign cyst, not a tumor, but he scheduled a BIOPSY just to be sure.*

bisque (bisk): a thick and creamy soup made from meat, fish, or shellfish.

> *Mom didn't care what else was on the menu, as long as the restaurant offered lobster BISQUE.*

bizarre (bih-ZAR): strange; incomprehensible; deviating from what is expected or in the rational order of things. (See, for comparison, the entry for *bazaar*.)

> *As the drug began to take effect, Bill began to make BIZARRE remarks about large insects and dancing toasters.*

blacklist (BLAK-list): to place on a list of disapproved or rejected persons and organizations.

> *Many prominent entertainment figures were BLACKLISTED in Hollywood for alleged ties with Communism.*

bloc (BLOK): a group of persons or nations with various political beliefs united for a common cause.

> *Former Eastern BLOC countries include Poland and Hungary.*

bluejacket (BLOO-jak-eht): a person enlisted in the United States or British Navy.

> *Because San Diego is a big Navy town, many of its nightclubs cater to BLUEJACKETS and attract few civilians.*

bogey (BOE-gie): in golf, to post a score of one stroke over par on a hole; an instance of such a score.

> *Jeff BOGEYED on the fourteenth hole.*

bogus (BOE-guss): fake; counterfeit.

> *Earnest-looking teens with obviously BOGUS IDs were nothing new to the area's liquor store owners; a six-year-old with a revolver demanding two quarts of Thunderbird was something else again.*

bombarded (bom-BARD-ud): under attack; also, peppered with queries, problems, accusations, etc.

> *During the final class before the midterm exam, Professor Strang was BOMBARDED with questions from her panicky students.*

bonhomie (bohn-uh-MEE): a pleasant disposition.

> *Bill's attempts at BONHOMIE were usually futile, limited to a curt and forced "hello" for each staff member as the day began.*

bon mot (bon moe): a clever or witty comment.

> *The secretary of state's well-timed BON MOT about the shortcomings of American beer helped to put everyone at ease at a tense moment of the summit meeting.*

bon vivant (bon vih-VAHNT): a person who enjoys living well.

> *In Paris with her rich aunt, Janice lived the life of a BON VIVANT, shopping and dining out to her heart's content.*

born (born): carried to term in childbirth; given birth. (See, for comparison, the entry for *borne*.)

> *My son David was BORN at about four in the afternoon.*

borne (born): supported; carried; brought forth or produced. (See, for comparison, the entry for *born*.)

> *"BORNE" is the past participle of the verb "to bear" in all senses that do not involve childbirth.*

bosky (BOS-kee): thick with underbrush; wooded.

> *Straying from the marked trail, the hikers soon found themselves lost in the BOSKY, uncharted wilderness.*

bough (bow): a branch of a tree. (See, for comparison, the entry for *bow*.)

> *The BOUGHS of the apple tree hung heavy with fruit.*

bow (bow): to bend low; to yield. (See, for comparison, the entry for *bough*.)

> *The Japanese ambassador BOWED in the direction of the prime minister.*

bouillabaisse (BOO-yuh-base): a stew made from various kinds of fish, usually shellfish.

> *After Uncle Charlie helped us clean the fish and clams we'd caught, Aunt Pattie showed us how to make her famous BOUILLABAISSE.*

bovine (BO-vine): of or resembling a cow or ox; dull.

> *The hardest part of teaching high school for me has been getting used to the look of BOVINE submissiveness on most of my students' faces.*

bowdlerize (BOWD-lur-ize): to "cleanse" or modify a work of literature (or art) by removing parts considered offensive or otherwise altering content and style.

> *Producers of* Gone With the Wind *refused to BOWDLERIZE Margaret Mitchell's famous line, "Frankly, my dear, I don't give a damn."*

brake (brake): to control or stop. (See, for comparison, the entry for *break.*)

> *The car's BRAKING ability was truly remarkable; it felt as though I could stop on a dime.*

break (brake): to crack; to damage or injure. (See, for comparison, the entry for *brake.*)

> *If you're not careful driving that car, young man, you'll get in an accident and BREAK your neck.*

bravura (bruh-VOOR-uh): an amazing or daring display of style, technique, or expertise; also, as a noun, a particularly difficult and showy passage in a piece of music requiring both technical proficiency and great energy on the part of the performer.

> *Ron Liebman's portrayal of attorney Roy Cohn was a BRAVURA performance, the kind that makes critics sit back in awe.*

brazen (BRAY-zun): bold or shameless in display; unconcerned with the reactions of others.

> *None of us understood how Julia and Ted, each of whom is married, could have been so BRAZEN about their romance.*

brazier (BRAY-zhur): A metal container for holding burning coals.

> *Sitting side by side in the cozy farm kitchen, we sipped hot cider and toasted muffins over the BRAZIER.*

breadth (bredth): the side-to-side extent of something; width; expanse. (See, for comparison, the entry for *breath.*)

> *The alley was so narrow that my car had a clearance of perhaps two inches beyond its BREADTH on either side.*

breath (breth): the process or act of breathing; an inhalation or exhalation. (see, for comparison, the entry for *breadth*.)

> *Take a deep BREATH; I'm about to give you some bad news.*

broach (broach): to bring up or put forth as a topic for discussion.

> *The evening with Dan was pleasant enough, probably because none of us had the courage to BROACH the subject of his impending indictment.*

brogue (BROAG): an Irish accent in spoken English.

> *Although Mrs. O'Leary left Ireland when she was a young girl, you can still detect a slight BROGUE in her speech.*

brooch (broach *or* brooch): an ornamental pin, usually large.

> *Christmas just wouldn't be Christmas without Aunt Gertrude in her green-flowered dress and ruby BROOCH.*

brouhaha (BROO-ha-ha): an event that involves or invokes excitement, turmoil, or conflict.

> *The BROUHAHA in the hotel lobby was the result of a rock star making his way from his limousine to the elevator.*

bucolic (byoo-KOL-ik): pastoral; rural or rustic in nature.

> *Deana's farm, with its blooming apple trees and peaceful brooks, was just the kind of BUCOLIC scene we had been hoping to photograph for our article.*

bulimia (buh-LEE-mee-uh): an eating disorder in which sufferers alternately binge, then purge, forcing themselves to vomit.

The faculty health center featured a nurse with special training in dealing with BULIMIA and other eating disorders.

bulwark (BULL-wurk): a wall made of earthen materials built as a defense mechanism; any extensive protective measure taken against external danger.

The money set aside in the emergency fund was regarded as a BULWARK against future disasters, to ensure that we would be prepared the next time.

burnout (BURN-out): a condition of fatigue, low morale, or frustration resulting from excessive stress or overwork.

Although Leland's family feared he would suffer BURNOUT if he continued to work fourteen hours a day, seven days a week, he seemed to be happier than anyone could remember seeing him.

bursar (BUR-ser): the treasurer of a college.

At the beginning of each semester the students receiving financial aid would line up outside the BURSAR's office to sign their student loan papers.

butte (BYOOT): a solitary hill on a large plain.

The mission was situated atop a lonely-looking BUTTE outside of town.

Byzantine (BIZ-un-teen): of or referring to the ornate, detailed architectural style developed in Byzantium during the 5th century A.D.; also, devious; also, exceptionally complex or minutely laid out.

> *The company's BYZANTINE organizational scheme sometimes left newcomers feeling that they reported to everyone in general and no one in particular.*

cache (kash): a place where things of value are hidden; also, the things stored there.

> *Elwood, a shrewd swindler, kept a CACHE of stock certificates, Swiss bank account numbers, and jewels just in case he had to leave the country in short order.*

cachet (kah-SHAY): a mark of distinction or originality.

> *Walter thought that the velvet smoking jacket lent him a certain CACHET that was in keeping with his image as a man of leisure.*

cacophony (kuh-KOFF-uh-nee): a sound that is harsh and unpleasant to the ears.

> *The CACOPHONY of the work crew's hammers, saws, and drills was not what I had in mind when I asked for a wake-up call.*

cadence (KAY-dence): the rhythm or flow of a series of words or sounds; often, the harmonious rhythm or flow of the spoken word.

> *The poem's CADENCE echoed the lazy summer days of the poet's youth.*

cajole (kuh-JOLE): to coax; to persuade by using flattery; to wheedle.

> *My brother's efforts to CAJOLE me out of my allowance, by reminding me that I would be a rich superstar in big-league baseball someday, were in vain.*

California (kal-ih-FORN-yuh): the thirty-first state of the United States.

> *The capital of CALIFORNIA is Sacramento.*

callous (KAL-uss): unfeeling; insensitive; hardened. (See, for comparison, the entry for *callus*.)

> *The chauffeur couldn't understand how Mr. Jensen could be so CALLOUS as to ride by the crowd of homeless people every day without taking the least notice of them.*

callow (KAL-oh): lacking experience; immature.

> *Ellis, a CALLOW youth accompanying Madame Hempstead, seemed not to understand that his joke about the Ambassador's choice of underwear was inappropriate for a state dinner.*

callus (KAL-us): a hardened patch of skin. (See, for comparison, the entry for *callous*.)

> *George had developed a CALLUS on his forefinger from his constant guitar playing.*

calumny (KAL-um-nee): a slanderous statement made with the intent of hurting another's reputation; a malicious rumor.

> *The columnist apparently thought that the CALUMNY she directed at Senator Martin would cause him to lose only the election, not his wife and family as well.*

calzone (kal-ZONE): an Italian food roll resembling a turnover made by wrapping meat, cheese, or vegetables in dough.

We asked Aunt Joan if she would bring her famous steak and cheese CALZONE to the party.

cambric (KAM-brik): a variety of fine linen.

My grandmother gave us a beautiful CAMBRIC tablecloth as a wedding present.

canapé (KAN-uh-pay): an appetizer made by spreading meat, fish, or cheese on a small piece of toasted bread.

While the guests waited for the bridal party, waiters strolled through the reception area with trays of champagne and CANAPÉS.

cannon (KAH-nun): a weapon used to fire large metal projectiles. (See, for comparison, the entry for *canon*.)

The thunderous sound of CANNONS being fired resonated across the valley.

canon (KAH-nun): a principle governing political or religious groups; a law or set of laws. (See, for comparison, the entry for *cannon*.)

Early in the play, Hamlet expresses his wish that God "had not fix'd his CANON 'gainst self-slaughter."

cantankerous (kan-TANG-ker-us): ill-tempered; grumpy.

"You kids stay off my lawn!" our CANTANKEROUS old neighbor barked.

canvas (KAN-vus): a type of coarse cloth. (See, for comparison, the entry for *canvass*.)

> *Many of Van Gogh's works were destroyed and sold as scrap CANVAS.*

canvass (KAN-vus): to solicit (support, opinions, votes, etc.). (See, for comparison, the entry for *canvas*.)

> *Virgil and I spent all Sunday walking around the city CANVASSING for our candidate.*

capital (KAP-ih-tul): a city designated as a seat of government. Also: economic resources. Also: excellent. (See, for comparison, the entry for *capitol*.)

> *In Washington D.C., our nation's CAPITAL, the three branches of government make their formal headquarters.*

capitol (KAP-ih-tul): the building in which a legislature meets. (See, for comparison, the entry for *capital*.)

> *One of the highlights of our trip to Washington was our visit to the CAPITOL building.*

carafe (kuh-RAFF): a wide-mouthed bottle for holding liquid.

> *I would have been happy with a single glass of the house wine, but Billy, who was in a generous mood, insisted we order a CARAFE of the expensive Chardonnay.*

carbuncle (KAR-bunk-uhl): a painful inflammation of the skin similar to, but more serious than, a boil.

> *Jimmy's inventive excuses for his absences reached a new level when he told his teacher he had been unable to attend Spanish class because of a CARBUNCLE.*

carcinogen (kar-SIN-uh-gen): an agent that causes cancer.

When experimenting with CARCINOGENS in the lab, the technicians would always wear protective masks.

cardiac (KAR-dee-ack): relating to the heart.

When their son's pediatrician detected a heart murmur, the Simpsons insisted on having him examined by the best CARDIAC team in the city.

careen (kuh-REEN): to lurch while moving; to swerve.

Suddenly we hit a patch of oil, and our car CAREENED into the guardrail.

carnivorous (kar-NIV-uh-russ): flesh-eating.

Mel and his photographer set off for three months in the Serengeti in search of the CARNIVOROUS wildlife of the region.

castigate (KASS-tuh-gate): to criticize or rebuke severely, usually with the intention of correcting wrongdoing.

The committee CASTIGATED the college's administration for unethical recruiting practices.

cataclysmic (kat-uh-KLIZ-mik): pertaining to a disastrous event; of or pertaining to a significant and violent event resulting in mass destruction.

In his predictions, Nostradamus seems to speak of a CATACLYSMIC world war leading to the extinction of life on earth as we know it.

catacomb (KAT-uh-kome): a chamber below the ground with openings for graves.

During times of religious persecution, early Christians often had to worship alongside the dead in the CATACOMBS.

catapult (KAT-uh-pult): to hurl or shoot (as from a sling); to provide or exhibit sudden upward movement. As a noun: an ancient military weapon designed to hurl arrows, stones, and other missiles.

When he heard the approaching sirens, Michael CATAPULTED out of bed.

catarrh (kuh-TARR): an inflammation of the mucous membrane, especially one affecting the throat or nose.

Dr. Alonzo promised us that his special elixir would relieve any and all illnesses, including influenza, CATARRH, and snakebite.

catharsis (kuh-THAR-siss): to purify and rejuvenate the body and spirit by purging them of whatever is causing problems; to release tensions and achieve renewal by an outpouring of emotion.

Jimmy's therapist suggested that the young boy take up painting as a means of achieving a CATHARSIS after his father's death.

catheter (KATH-uh-tur): a slim, flexible tube inserted in a bodily channel to maintain an opening to another internal opening.

The endless months in my hospital room took their toll on my spirits; one morning I contemplated tearing the CATHETER from my arm, grabbing a bathrobe, and simply stalking out of the place.

cavort (kuh-VORT): to caper about; to prance.

Elwood and Riley were so happy to be released from the kennel that they spent half an hour CAVORTING wildly about on our lawn.

CD-ROM (see-dee-ROM): of or pertaining to a computer system employing compact discs as an information medium—rather than, or in addition to, standard disk media. (The letters stand for "compact disk/read-only memory.")

The software, which features superb graphics and stereo sound, is available only in CD-ROM format.

cede (seed): to give up, as by treaty.

In 1819, Spain CEDED to the United States the territory we now know as the state of Florida.

celestial (suh-LESS-chul): relating to the skies or the heavens.

At first Sam thought that the CELESTIAL body he had picked up on his telescope was a spaceship, but it turned out to be a meteor.

censer (SEN-sur): a vessel for burning incense. (See, for comparison, the entry for *censor.*)

Father Riley looked in vain for the altar boy, then placed the CENSER on the altar himself.

censor (SEN-sur): one who reviews for offensive or objectionable material, deleting that which is found to fall into such categories. (See, for comparison, the entry for *censer.*)

W.C. Fields was constantly at odds with Hays Commission CENSORS, who found fault with many of his references to alcohol and women.

censorious (sen-SOR-ee-us): critical; easily finding fault.

When it came to grading term papers, Mrs. Edwards was seen by many as overly CENSORIOUS, even taking off points for using a paper clip instead of a staple.

cerebellum (sare-uh-BELL-um): a region of the brain located the back of the cerebrum and the brain stem; the portion of the brain concerned with muscle coordination and bodily equilibrium.

Mary's frequent dizziness after the car accident led doctors to believe that there might have been an injury to her CEREBELLUM.

cerebral (suh-REEB-rul): appealing to or involving the human mind; characteristic of intellectual pursuits; also, pertaining to the brain.

Bill's lofty observations on the nature of existence are a little too CEREBRAL for a party like this; you'd be better off inviting Charlie, who tells such funny stories.

chafe (chayf): to rub or irritate. (See, for comparison, the entry for *chaff.*)

The new shoes CHAFED my heels the first day and left me with two prize-winning blisters.

chaff (chaff): worthless stuff; material to be cast away. (See, for comparison, the entry for *chafe.*)

I usually write for an hour straight in my journal, knowing full well that much of what comes out will be drivel, and allowing myself to go back later and separate the wheat from the CHAFF.

chalet (sha-LAY): a small country house, named after a type of Swiss cottage with overhanging eaves.

> *We rented a CHALET on the edge of the mountain, and had immediate access to the ski slopes.*

chameleon (kuh-MEE-lee-un): a lizard (*chameleontidae* and similar animals) with the ability to change the color of its skin for the purpose of camouflage; also, a person who shifts outlooks, opinions, or identities frequently or easily.

> *I'm afraid we haven't been able to get Ian to give us his final opinion on the merger plans; he's been something of a CHAMELEON on the issue.*

chanteuse (shan-TEUZ): a female singer, usually one who performs in nightclubs.

> *Although he claimed to like the decor and the atmosphere of the club, we suspected that Elaine, the CHANTEUSE who performed there, was the real reason Jimmy kept going back.*

chantey (SHAN-tee): a song sung by sailors in rhythm to their labors.

> *As they hauled up anchor, the ship's crew would join together in "What Shall We Do with a Drunken Sailor" and other CHANTEYS.*

chasm (KAZ-um): a deep gorge; a deep hole in the earth's surface.

> *Dawn stood peering across the seemingly bottomless CHASM, meditating on the mysteries of nature.*

chateau (sha-TOE): a large country house; a French manor house or castle.

> *Eva liked to spend her summers at the family's CHATEAU, strolling through the gardens and riding horseback over the expansive grounds.*

chemotherapy (kee-mo-THARE-uh-pee): the treatment of disease by means of administering chemicals that have a toxic effect on the microorganisms that cause the disease, or that can destroy a body's cancerous cells.

> *The doctors warned Amelia that the CHEMOTHERAPY she was about to undergo would not be without side effects.*

chide (chide): to scold or lecture; to reprove.

> *My brother CHIDED me for neglecting to visit our grandparents during my trip to California.*

chintzy (CHINT-see): considered cheap, tacky, or of low quality.

> *Angela insisted on wearing a CHINTZY leopard-skin jumpsuit and high heels to the company Christmas party.*

chloroform (KLORE-uh-form): a colorless, toxic liquid chemical possessing a strong ether smell, and sometimes used as an anesthetic.

> *Police found a CHLOROFORM soaked-rag on the floor of the study and surmised that the kidnappers had used it to knock Mr. Robinson out.*

chord (kord): a combination of musical tones. (See, for comparison, the entry for *cord*.)

> *The major CHORDS in the key of C are the easiest for the beginning piano student to learn.*

churlish (CHUR-lish): ill-bred; boorish.

> *When he started drinking soup noisily straight from the bowl, Beverly decided she had seen enough of her blind date's CHURLISH behavior.*

cinematic (sin-uh-MAT-ik): reminiscent of or pertaining to the cinema; similar in imagery or approach to the visual styles employed in motion pictures.

> *The use of a large rotating disk on the stage allows the director to stage scenes in such a way that scenery and actors pass steadily across the stage as action proceeds, lending a CINEMATIC feel to the performance.*

cipher (SIE-fur): a person or thing without meaning or value; a mystery; literally, the mathematical symbol for zero.

> *Despite the best efforts of the intelligence community to gather evidence against him, Doctor Lysenko remained a CIPHER.*

circa (SUR-ka): an estimated historical time period.

> *Based on the diary's condition, as well as the handwriting style and vocabulary choices of its author, Professor Evans set the date at CIRCA 1910.*

circumflex (SUR-kum-flex): an accent mark (^) placed over a letter to indicate a certain pronunciation.

> *Much to the dismay of the European journalists in town to cover the road race, the American typewriters in their hotels had no keys for CIRCUMFLEXES or other accent marks.*

circumlocution (sur-kum-lo-KYOO-shun): an instance of using more words than necessary to express a thought; the act of avoiding touching on an issue directly by means of skirting it with the use of many words.

> *Tired of Peter's CIRCUMLOCUTION, I interrupted him and asked him if he wanted me to go out on a date with him.*

circumspect (SUR-kum-spekt): wary of consequences.

> *Having been stung once, Ferdinand was CIRCUMSPECT about where he sat, and always checked for bees.*

cistern (SIS-tern): a large container or tank used for holding water, particularly rainwater.

> *Mary watered her garden with rainwater collected in a CISTERN behind the garage.*

cite (site): to quote or refer to. (See, for comparison, the entry for *site*.)

> *I've CITED your brilliant paper several times in my upcoming book, Dr. Wilson.*

citify (SIT-uh-fie): to cause to become city-like.

> *I'm afraid it will take more than a week in Chicago to CITIFY old Uncle Parker.*

claque (KLAK): a group of people hired to applaud at an entertainment event.

> *The first comedian was absolutely terrible; if it hadn't been for the CLAQUE the management had assembled at the last minute, there wouldn't have been any applause at all.*

climactic (klie-MAK-tik): of or pertaining to a climax. (See, for comparison, the entry for *climatic*.)

> *The CLIMACTIC moment of the play comes when Hamlet finally kills Claudius.*

climatic (klie-MAT-ik): of or pertaining to climate. (See, for comparison, the entry for *climactic*.)

> *The CLIMATIC conditions in northern Alberta during the winter really don't agree with me.*

clinch (klinch): to settle a matter decisively or definitely. Also, as a noun: a passionate embrace.

> *Even Coach Jones admitted that his team had slacked off after they CLINCHED first place in their division.*

cloistered (KLOI-sturd): secluded; isolated; removed or hidden.

> *Shocked by the news of the shooting on our street, we remained CLOISTERED in our house for days afterward.*

coagulate (ko-AG-yoo-late): to change from a liquid to a solid-like mass.

> *As someone who claims to be qualified to teach high school biology, you should certainly be able to answer a question on what makes blood COAGULATE.*

coda (KO-duh): in music, the final passage of a movement or piece; also, the final part of anything, especially an artistic work.

> *As the "experimental" orchestral piece finally reached its CODA, I saw the percussionist yawn and look at his watch.*

codger (KOD-jur): a peculiar or eccentric man, generally of advanced years.

> *Our next-door neighbor was Mr. Pottman, a likeable CODGER who used to wash his car every afternoon, even if it had rained in the morning.*

cogitate (KOJ-ih-tate): to think about or ponder seriously.

> *The president, never one to be pressured into a decision, closed the discussion by saying he needed another week to COGITATE on the matter.*

cognizant (KOG-nuh-zunt): aware or well informed.

> *The attorney angrily denied the charges that his client had been COGNIZANT of the scheme to defraud consumers.*

cognomen (kog-NO-muhn): a nickname.

> *He doesn't mind being called "Leopold," but he prefers his COGNOMEN, "Lee."*

cognoscente (kon-yuh-SHEN-tee): a connoisseur; an expert. (Plural: cognoscenti.)

> *When it comes to wine-tasting, Arthur is well respected as a COGNOSCENTE.*

coiffure (kwa-FYOOR): a hairdo; the style of one's hair.

> *When you're as rich and powerful as Don King. I imagine you can get away with wearing any COIFFURE you like.*

coitus (KO-uh-tus): sexual intercourse.

> *Professor Wells sternly informed me that he would prefer that I use the term "COITUS" in describing the activities of the test couples, rather than the less formal "making whoopee."*

collate (KOE-late): to arrange (usually paper) in proper or logical order.

> *Chef LeBlanc's assistant was responsible for writing down the recipes and COLLATING them for inclusion in the restaurant's internal cookbook.*

collateral (kuh-LAT-uh-rul): something pledged as security or insurance for the fulfillment of an obligation or payment. (Also, as an adjective: secondary or accompanying.)

> *Sheila offered her house as COLLATERAL in order to obtain the loan she needed to start her business.*

Colorado: (koll-uh-RAH-doe): the thirty-eighth state of the United States.

> *The capital of COLORADO is Denver.*

combustible (kum-BUS-tih-bul): susceptible to catching fire; able to be burned.

> *The local consumer group tried to help make neighborhood homes as safe as possible by publishing lists of products found to be poisonous, COMBUSTIBLE, or potentially hazardous to small children.*

comity (KOM-ih-tee): courtesy; mutual civility.

> *The police were kind enough to grant me the COMITY of a private telephone call once I promised to stop removing pieces of clothing and flinging them at the sergeant.*

comme ci, comme ça (kum SEE kum SA): middling; neither extraordinarily good nor extraordinarily poor. (French for "like this, like that.")

> *"COMME CI, COMME ÇA," shrugged Wells when I asked him how he was doing.*

commemorate (kum-MEM-uh-rate): to serve as a memorial for; to mark or celebrate as a significant event.

> *Arthur, a Korean War veteran, would COMMEMORATE Memorial Day by visiting the cemetery and placing flags on the graves of friends who had fallen in battle.*

commodious (kuh-MODE-ee-uss): spacious; roomy.

> *Mr. and Mrs. Davis found the five-bedroom house a much more COMMODIOUS abode for their family of four than the apartment had been.*

compensate (KOM-pun-sate): something given in return for or to make up for services performed, or for something lost; something given in exchange.

> *Although management COMPENSATED George for crossing the picket line during the strike by giving him a promotion and a big raise, he had lost several friends as a result of his decision and regretted it bitterly.*

compile (kum-PILE): to gather or put together in one place or form.

> *The disc jockey asked Janet and Peter to COMPILE a list of the songs they would most like to hear at their wedding.*

complacent (kum-PLAY-sent): satisfied with oneself; smug; content.

> *Brian was so COMPLACENT during the practice scrimmages before the big game that his coach considered benching him and playing the backup quarterback instead.*

complement (KOM-pluh-munt): to accompany in a pleasing or harmonious style. Also, as a noun: something that completes or brings to perfection. (See, for comparison, the entry for *compliment*.)

> *That scarf you're wearing certainly COMPLEMENTS your blouse.*

complementary (kom-pluh-MEN-tuh-ree): serving to complete or to accompany in a harmonious fashion. (See, for comparison, the entry for *complimentary*.)

> *The trick is to pick a living room style COMPLEMENTARY to the one we've already established in the kitchen.*

compliant (kum-PLY-ant): submissive; yielding.

> *After we phoned the police a few times, our noisy neighbor found it in his heart to be more COMPLIANT when we asked him to keep down the racket.*

complicity: to be involved in or be associated with, or to participate in or have previous knowledge of, an instance of wrongdoing.

> *Although he did not receive money for throwing the 1919 World Series, Buck Weaver was nevertheless suspended from baseball for life, because his failure to expose the scheme was seen as COMPLICITY in his teammates' plans.*

compliment (KOM-pluh-munt): to praise or flatter. (See, for comparison, the entry for *complement*.)

> *The waiter COMPLIMENTED Harry on his choice of wine.*

complimentary (kom-pluh-MEN-tuh-ree): expressing praise or admiration; also, extended without charge. (See, for comparison, the entry for *complementary*.)

> *The play was uneven and only mildly interesting, but I couldn't complain too much, as the tickets had been COMPLIMENTARY.*

compose (kum-POZE): to be the constituent components of; to make up. (See, for comparison, the entry for *comprise*.)

> *Teamwork COMPOSES the essence of success in business.*

compote (KOM-poat): a stewed fruit and sugar dessert.

> *In addition to an unidentifiable brownish meat in a dark, concealing sauce, many of the TV dinners I ate as a child included a rather leaden strawberry COMPOTE.*

comprise (kum-PRIZE): to include or contain; to consist of. (See, for comparison, the entry for *compose*.)

> *The new complex COMPRISES several floors of student residences, a cafeteria, and a recreation area.*

concave (kahn-CAVE): curving inward, as the inside of a sphere. (See, for comparison, the entry for *convex*.)

> *After Bill threw it in anger, the baseball left a CONCAVE impression in the wall.*

concede (kun-SEED): to admit or acknowledge the truth or validity of.

> *"You were right," our broker CONCEDED, "we should have sold those shares last month."*

concise (kun-SICE): clear and to the point; brief; expressing much with few words.

> *Rather than detail the grievances he had with his supervisor, Randy handed in a CONCISE resignation letter outlining his desire to move on to something new.*

conclave (KON-klave): a secret meeting; also, the room in which this meeting is held.

> *Fearing he might crack under pressure, the rebels did not include Eli in the CONCLAVE in which they gathered to plan their attack strategy.*

concoct (kun-KOKT): to combine in the process of preparation.

> *How on earth did Myra manage to CONCOCT a story like that for her mother on such short notice?*

concur (kun-KUR): to agree; to share the same opinion.

> *The prosecutor felt that Jim's crime deserved the maximum penalty, but the judge did not CONCUR.*

condensed (kun-DENSED): shortened; decreased in size; compressed, made more concise.

> *Cindy thought she could get through the class by reading only the CONDENSED versions of the novels that had been assigned, but she ended up failing both the midterm and the final.*

confiscate (KON-fiss-kate): to deprive of (one's property), especially as part of an official or governmental body.

> *The news that his boat had been CONFISCATED by the IRS to satisfy his back tax debt hit Michael like a body blow.*

conform (kun-FORM): to go along with what is popular; to follow the actions of others. Also: not to be in violation of (a rule, principle, ideal, or edict).

> *As though eager to prove she had no intention of CONFORMING to her parents' idea of the perfect daughter, Bridget left home at eighteen to become a truck driver.*

confraternity (kahn-fruh-TURN-ih-tee): an association of people united for a common cause.

> *Eager to improve the condition of our neighborhood playgrounds, Carol and I joined a town CONFRATERNITY that had formed for that purpose.*

Connecticut (kuh-NET-ih-kut): the fifth state of the United States.

> *The capital of CONNECTICUT is Hartford.*

connote (kuh-NOTE): to imply, suggest, or hint at another meaning in addition to a primary one.

> *To many people the term "frontier" CONNOTES a rough and primitive lifestyle, but most pioneer families maintained household living standards that equaled those of the eastern relatives they'd left behind.*

consensus (kun-SEN-sus): collective agreement.

> *There was a strong consensus around town was that Mayor Bergeron was doing a poor job—a CONSENSUS that extended to both of his children, his uncles, and his barber.*

conspicuous (kun-SPIK-yoo-uss): strikingly noticeable; obvious.

> *The present Supreme Court term has been marked by a CONSPICUOUS absence of controversial cases.*

conspiracy (kun-SPEER-uh-see): a treacherous plan involving two or more persons.

Your contention that Lyndon Johnson was part of a CONSPIRACY to assassinate President Kennedy amounts to what, in an earlier day, would have been called seditious libel, Mr. Oliver.

constant dollars (KON-stuhnt DOLL-urz): in economics, a measure of monetary value in which the factors of inflation and deflation are accounted for; a base year's currency value used to determine what costs would presumably have been in other years.

The figures on our division's growth were extremely misleading because they had not been converted to CONSTANT DOLLARS.

construe (kun-STROO): to interpret or guess the meaning of.

Ann's constant tardiness was CONSTRUED by her supervisor as an inability to balance the demands of her job and her family.

contiguous (kun-TIG-yoo-uss): joining physically; touching.

The prize offer is limited to residents of the forty-eight CONTIGUOUS states.

contravention (kon-truh-VEN-shun): an instance of contradiction or opposition; also, the condition of being overruled or disobeyed.

Your appearance here without the full report is in blatant CONTRAVENTION of the instructions laid out in my memo.

contrite (kun-TRITE): inclined to express penitence or apology.

> *Myrtle's CONTRITE speech did little to mitigate her supervisor's frustration at the delay in the release of the Model X.*

controvert (KON-truh-vert): to oppose with logical reasoning; to dispute or contradict.

> *No matter how many attempts the defense makes to CONTROVERT the details of this sequence of events, the fact remains that the defendant was seen leaving the building immediately after the murder.*

convene (kun-VEEN): to gather or assemble.

> *The legislature will not CONVENE this year until February 1.*

convex (kon-VEX): curving outward, as the outside of a sphere. (See, for comparison, the entry for *concave*.)

> *Little Stephen laughed as he watched the tiny car plunge off the CONVEX surface of his large toy ball.*

cord (kord): a thin piece of rope, plastic, etc. (See, for comparison, the entry for *chord*.)

> *Today's rock artists are used to performing with microphones that do not require CORDS.*

cordial (KORD-jull): pleasant; marked by warmth or kindness.

> *The Fords extended a CORDIAL welcome to us as we arrived for the party.*

corollary (KORE-uh-lare-ee): accompanying element; consequence; thing brought about as a result (of some factor).

> *The natural COROLLARY of your theory that Hawkins murdered his mistress to silence her would appear to be that she had told him she was about to go public with details of their affair.*

corporal (KOR-puh-rul): related to the body. Also: a military rank. (See, for comparison, the entry for *corporeal*.)

> *The school has a strict policy forbidding CORPORAL punishment.*

corporeal (kor-PORE-ee-ul): tangible; having material existence. (See, for comparison, the entry for *corporal*.)

> *The estate sold the late author's CORPOREAL assets, but it retained the copyright of all his intellectual properties, both published and unpublished.*

corpulent (KORP-you-lunt): obese; fat; bulky.

> *A CORPULENT waiter, apparently meant to frighten us into sensible eating, waddled out to ask us whether we were interested in hearing about the restaurant's special low-calorie entrees.*

correlate (KORE-uh-late): to relate logically or systematically; to link; as a noun (KORE-uh-lut), something correlated to something else.

> *I believe I can demonstrate convincingly that the increased cancer rate in the town is directly CORRELATED to the dumping practices of your firm over the past twenty years.*

corrigendum (kor-ih-JEHN-dum): an error to be corrected in a manuscript. (Plural: corrigenda.)

> *The proofreader handed the manuscript back to Bill, who was horrified to find that it still contained hundreds of CORRIGENDA.*

cosmic (KOZ-mik): of or pertaining to the universe as a whole; also, far-reaching or pervasive.

> *It is my hope that the council will use our report as a blueprint for COSMIC, rather than cosmetic, changes in city government.*

council (KOWN-sul): an assembly gathered together for deliberation or consultation.

> *The neighborhood COUNCIL meets every Tuesday night to discuss issues of interest to our community.*

counsel (KOWN-sul): a discussion of ideas or opinions.

> *Katrina's advisor was always available to COUNSEL her about work-related issues.*

countervail (kown-tur-VAIL): to use equal force against; to compensate.

> *The challenger hit the champion with two quick left jabs and a right uppercut, but the champion COUNTERVAILED with a left hook.*

coup de grace (koo duh GRAHCE): a decisive act or event that brings a situation to a close; the finishing blow.

> *The COUP DE GRACE came when Paul threw his bowl of oatmeal at Mona's feet, leading her to reevaluate their relationship.*

couplet (KUP-lut): in poetry, two related lines, similar in rhyme or rhythm.

The use of the rhymed COUPLET at the end of a scene is a stock technique employed by Elizabethan playwrights to alert the audience to an upcoming shift in the action.

crag (KRAGG): a steep rock formation rising higher than its surrounding rocks.

Because this was my first rock-climbing experience, I regarded the huge CRAG we were approaching with some nervousness.

credible (KRED-ih-bul): worthy of belief; plausible. (See, for comparison, the entry for *creditable.*)

The prosecution's witnesses seemed forthright and CREDIBLE, while those of the defense weren't quite as believable.

creditable (KRED-ih-tuh-bull): worthy of praise. (See, for comparison, the entry for *credible.*)

You've done a CREDITABLE job on this project, Farnsworth; remind me to give you a raise.

crescendo (kruh-SHEN-doe): a gradual increase in volume or intensity to a certain point (used especially in relation to musical works).

As the orchestra reached a thundering CRESCENDO, my six-year-old son continued to sleep peacefully by my side.

crestfallen (KREST-fall-uhn): in low spirits; extremely depressed.

When I heard that Marla would have to work late that evening, I was CRESTFALLEN.

criterion (krie-TEER-ee-un): standards; qualities or preconditions that must be met. Plural: criteria.

> *Stan met all of the college's CRITERIA for admission, but he put off applying because he simply didn't believe he was smart enough to survive there.*

croissant (kruh-SONT or kwa-SON): a crescent-shaped roll or pastry, sometimes prepared with a sweet or savory filling.

> *For Ellen, the CROISSANTS and fresh-squeezed orange juice were about the only things that made the company's breakfast meetings bearable.*

cryptic (KRIP-tik): secret; coded; concealed from open understanding.

> *After making a few CRYPTIC comments on the impermanence of all artistic effort, Melody slunk into her room; we learned in the morning that she had burned every page of her manuscript.*

cubism (KYOO-biz-um): a school of sculpture and painting that came to prominence in the early twentieth century in which forms are rendered as geometric structures.

> *Although Picasso is the first painter most people think of when asked to name a pioneer of CUBISM, his friend George Braque was equally important in the development of the movement.*

cubit (KYOO-bit): an archaic unit of measure, roughly equivalent to twenty inches.

> *Most editions of the Book of Genesis give the measurements of Noah's Ark in CUBITS, although some editors have converted such passages to modern terms of measurement.*

culinary (KYOO-lih-nar-ee): relating to cooking or the preparation of food.

My CULINARY efforts these days are much humbler than my library of cookbooks would lead you to believe.

cull (kull): to assemble or collect bit by bit; to select.

Having CULLED the most impressive poems from her early work, Ariel felt she was ready to submit the collection for publication.

curriculum (KUH-rik-yuh-lum): the courses of study, educational plan, or study path of a learning institution.

The history department here offers a solid, challenging CURRICULUM equal to that of the more prestigious Ivy League schools—and at a fraction of the cost.

cursory (KUR-suh-ree): performed with haste and without care.

Mrs. Wallace avoided giving tests on the Friday before a vacation, as she knew her students' efforts would be CURSORY at best.

curtail (ker-TALE): to abridge or truncate; to lessen, usually by taking or cutting away from.

His new office's 8:00 a.m. meetings meant Dwight would have to CURTAIL his late-night television watching.

cusp (kusp): a point formed by the intersection of two curves.

Just above the CUSP of the arch was a hook meant to hold a hanging plant.

cygnet (SIG-nit): A young swan.

The proud mother swan led her brood of CYGNETS toward the north end of the pond.

dandle (DAN-dull): to bounce (a child) on one's knees or in one's arms.

To calm the baby down, Aunt Irene DANDLED her on her knee and sang nursery rhymes.

daub (dawb): to smear with a sticky substance; to paint a surface in a hurried fashion.

I can see you've DAUBED a little black grease paint under your nose, Frank, but I'm afraid a good Groucho costume will require more than that.

dauntless (DAWNT-luss): unable to be intimidated or put down, brave; fearless.

Although Jan had told Michael she would never marry him, he was a DAUNTLESS suitor, sending flowers and candy on a daily basis.

dawdle (DAW-dull): to waste time; to loiter or loaf.

"If you don't stop DAWDLING, " Mrs. Adams scolded her husband, "we'll be late for the opera."

deadlock (DED-lok): an impasse resulting from two opposing and resistant forces.

With one member absent due to illness, the council found itself facing a four-to-four DEADLOCK after nearly two days of debate on the measure.

debug (dee-BUG): to remove errors from (a computer program).

> *Although the initial programming work was complete, Aaron anticipated that the DEBUGGING process would be long and arduous.*

debutante (DEB-yoo-tont): a young woman making her debut into society; any unmarried young woman perceived to move in high social circles.

> *Amanda and her friends scanned the newspaper's society column for a review of their DEBUTANTE ball.*

decanter (dih-CAN-ter): a fancy glass bottle used for serving wine, brandy, etc.

> *As teenagers, Austin and Billy would sometimes steal wine from the DECANTER in the den, replacing it with fruit juice.*

decapitate (dee-KAP-ih-tate): to remove the head of.

> *Although the guillotine was initially proposed as a humane method of execution, the idea of using a machine to DECAPITATE criminals now strikes most people as barbaric.*

decasyllabic (dek-uh-sil-LAB-ik): in verse, having ten syllables in one line.

> *The epic poem followed a DECASYLLABIC form.*

decipher (dih-CIE-fur): to figure out or make sense of; to get the meaning of (particularly with relation to ancient or difficult writing).

> *"If we can DECIPHER the symbols on these scrolls," said the archaeologist, "I believe we'll know exactly where to look for the tomb."*

decree (dih-KREE): an official order or announcement, especially from the government or another recognized authority, that settles a matter with finality; also, to issue such an order.

> *The DECREE mandating integration of public schools set off one of the most bitterly divisive conflicts in the town's history.*

deem (deem): to judge; to regard or assess.

> *For reasons the writer could not fathom, his boardroom scene, which contained no nudity or violence and only the mildest language, was DEEMED unsuitable for network broadcast.*

deface (dih-FACE): to disfigure or damage.

> *It breaks my heart to see the old stone bridge, my one unchanging companion from boyhood, DEFACED with the spraypainted grumblings of drunken teenagers.*

de facto (dih FAK-toe): in fact; actual.

> *The death of the prime minister left Jones, for the moment, the DE FACTO leader of the nation.*

defalcate (dih-FAL-kate): to embezzle.

> *No one knew for certain how the corrupt banker had made his fortune, but it was rumored that he had DEFALCATED funds from a bogus charitable organization.*

defer (dih-FUR): to delay or put off until another time; also, to yield with respect.

> *With regard to the scheduling of our announcement, I DEFER to my friend the chairman.*

defeatist (dih-FEET-ist): accepting defeat as an unavoidable consequence of life; pessimistic.

> *Sheldon's DEFEATIST attitude led Monica, his supervisor, to wonder whether he would ever complete the project he was working on.*

deficient (dih-FISH-unt): lacking.

> *As a result of a diet DEFICIENT in calcium, Cathy's fingernails were very thin and easily broken.*

defile (dih-FILE): to pollute; to corrupt or make unclean.

> *The river that only a few years ago ran clean and clear is now DEFILED with a witches' brew of chemicals, thanks to the new tanning plant.*

defunct (dih-FUNGKT): no longer in existence; obsolete; not living.

> *After the market crashed, my grandfather learned that the company he had worked for was suddenly DEFUNCT.*

deign (dane): to condescend; to lower oneself to a position or role considered unsuitable.

> *Since Walter won that writing prize, he hasn't DEIGNED to return any of my phone calls.*

delete (duh-LEET): to leave out or omit.

> *After a brief discussion with the principal, the members of the booster club decided to DELETE the section of their cheer that questioned the ancestry of the coach of the Brentwater football team.*

delft (delft): a kind of glazed earthenware featuring blue and white patterns.

> *My mother's gift of DELFT cookware complemented our blue and white kitchen beautifully.*

Delaware (DELL-uh-ware): the first state of the United States.

> *The capital of DELAWARE is Dover.*

dell (dell): a small wooded valley; a glen.

> *I emerged from the tent in the wee hours of the morning to find a sand-colored doe peering at me from the edge of the DELL.*

deluge (DELL-yoodje): a great flood or heavy rain; an overwhelming inundation of anything.

> *As the newest member of the accounting firm, Fred was unprepared for the DELUGE of tax returns that landed on his desk two weeks before the April 15 deadline.*

demerit (dih-MARE-it): a mark resulting in a loss of privilege for an offender.

> *Max received five DEMERITS from Mrs. Collins for his constant tardiness.*

demur (dih-MUR): to take exception; to object, particularly as a result of deeply held principles.

> *Mike suggested that we run an ad alluding to our opponent's supposed ties to organized crime, but Congressman Taylor DEMURRED.*

denigrate (DEN-ih-grate): to defame or speak ill of; literally, to blacken (a reputation, for instance).

Reprinting, without permission, the cruder poems of the writer's formative years was one strategy the reviewer used to DENIGRATE her entire body of work.

denizen (DEN-ih-zun): an inhabitant or resident.

Michael regarded homeless people as DENIZENS of another world until a series of setbacks landed him unexpectedly on the street.

dentifrice (DEN-ti-friss): any substance used to clean the teeth.

Dr. Sanchez gave me a lecture on the proper use of DENTIFRICES, and recommended several brands I could purchase in any supermarket.

deplete (dih-PLEET): to use up completely; to exhaust.

Once the coal deposits in the valley had been DEPLETED, the town of Harlenville, which had thrived for thirty years, virtually ceased to exist.

depose (dih-POZE): to oust or remove from office or a position of power and authority; also, to take testimony from someone under oath.

After the dictator was DEPOSED, the country set about healing the wounds of a long civil war.

depreciation (dih-pree-shee-AY-shun): a decrease in value, quality, or power, particularly due to wear or age.

Thanks to five years of DEPRECIATION, I couldn't get more than $2,000 for that car if I took it back to the dealer now.

deride (dih-RIDE): to ridicule with cruelty; to laugh at and make fun of.

His classmates DERIDED Joe for wearing argyle socks to the prom.

de rigueur (deuh rih-GER): required by etiquette; in good taste or form.

Since black tie and tails were DE RIGUEUR for the social events his new wife attended regularly, Julian found himself buying a tuxedo for the first time in his life.

derogatory (dih-ROG-uh-tore-ee): tending to lessen or impair someone or something; disparaging and negative.

Butch's DEROGATORY remarks about my girlfriend were meant to goad me into a fight, but I was determined to keep my cool.

derring-do (DARE-ing-DOO): heroic deeds; acts of bravery.

Luke Skywalker's challenges and feats of DERRING-DO are perhaps the most memorable elements of the Star Warstrilogy.

descry (dih-SKRIE): to spot as a result of attentive observation; to discover or find.

With mingled relief and dread the crew learned that the lookout had DESCRIED the white whale Ahab had been hunting.

desiccate (DESS-ih-late): to cause to dry out.

The food preparation process for the items to be taken on the astronauts' voyage involved elaborate DESICCATING and sanitation procedures.

designate (DEZ-ig-nate): to indicate; to point out or specify.

> *The Walker sisters DESIGNATED the last Thursday of each month as their evening to leave their husbands at home and go out to dinner together.*

detain (dih-TANE): to delay; to keep from going on; to confine.

> *The border police DETAINED the pair for two hours while they searched every inch of their vehicle for narcotics.*

determinism (dih-TUR-mun-iz-um): the belief that a person's course of action is not free but predetermined by external circumstances.

> *A true disciple of DETERMINISM, Jerry felt he should not be held accountable for having married three women—since, as he argued, each of the relationships had been "meant to be."*

detrimental (det-rih-MEN-tul): damaging or harmful in effect.

> *Your husband's cruel words to the children will prove DETRIMENTAL to his cause during the custody hearing.*

deviate (DEE-vee-ate): to turn away from or go off course; change course or direction. As a noun (DEE-vee-ut): a person who departs from the standard or norm.

> *My daughter's choice to wear cowboy boots with her wedding gown certainly DEVIATED from my standards of propriety, but there was no changing her mind.*

devoid (dih-VOID): lacking utterly; without.

> *"No matter how skilled a surgeon you become," Dr. Smith told the intern, "you'll fail as a doctor if you continue to be DEVOID of compassion and sympathy for patients."*

dexterity (dek-STARE-ih-tee): adroitness; the quality of being skilled in using one's hands and body.

> *I couldn't hit a jump-shot to save my life, but my speed, DEXTERITY, and passing ability made me a valuable member of the varsity basketball team.*

diadem (DIE-uh-dem): a royal crown.

> *The princess arrived at the state banquet wearing a DIADEM of emeralds and diamonds.*

dialect (DIE-uh-lekt): the aspects of a language (grammar, pronunciation, and vocabulary, for instance) particular to a geographic region.

> *Armed with four years of high school Spanish, I set out confidently on my vacation to Madrid—only to find myself adrift in a sea of incomprehensible DIALECTS on my arrival.*

digress (die-GRESS): to wander off the point of a discourse or conversation; to turn away from a course.

> *The topic of the speech was interesting enough, but Bill had an unfortunate habit of DIGRESSING from his text with irrelevant off-the-cuff stories.*

dilate (DIE-late): to expand.

> *The rock star's DILATED pupils led some to believe that he had been experimenting again with narcotics, and quite recently.*

diminish (dih-MIN-ish): to cause to be smaller; to decrease in size or importance.

> *In pointing out these problems, I don't mean for a moment to DIMINISH the achievements of your department this year.*

71

dionysian (die-uh—NIH-shun): relating to Dionysius, a Greek god of revelry; reminiscent of or pertaining to frenzied, uninhibited, or hedonistic behavior.

> *The fraternity's DIONYSIAN exploits were fun for a while, but when they resulted in his failing two classes, Emmett decided to go back to the quiet life.*

diorama (di-uh-RA-mah): A small model of a scene featuring painted figures and backgrounds.

> *Using a cardboard box, paint, and plaster of Paris, Frank helped his son construct a working DIORAMA of a corner store for a school art project.*

diphthong (DIF-thawng): a sound made by smoothly pronouncing two vowel sounds within one syllable.

> *English is full of DIPHTHONGS, examples of which can be found in such words as boil, house, and smile.*

dirge (durj): a funeral song; a song of mourning.

> *The DIRGE from Cymbeline, according to Professor Alpert, is the only worthwhile passage to be found in that seldom-produced Shakespeare play.*

disburse (dis-BURSE): to pay out; to expend.

> *After meeting with the president, our comptroller was finally authorized to DISBURSE the funds.*

discerning (Dis-SURN-ing): insightful; sound in evaluation or judgment.

> *Although Jamie is excellent at acquiring reference works, she is not the most DISCERNING editor when it comes to evaluating children's book proposals.*

disconsolate (dis-KON-suh-lut); beyond consolation; unable to be comforted; deep in grief or sorrow.

Jamie was DISCONSOLATE after missing what should have been the game-winning field goal.

discordant (dis-KOR-dunt): conflicting; lacking in harmony.

I find that composer's DISCORDANT style difficult to listen to.

discreet (dis-KREET): displaying or possessing tact and restraint in behavior and speech.

Mel felt his mother had been less than DISCREET in marrying Claude so soon after her first husband's funeral, and that she could easily have waited six months or so rather than three weeks.

discrepancy (dis-KREP-un-see): inconsistency; an instance of disagreement or difference.

John was the only one to notice the DISCREPANCY between the cash register receipts and the amount of money in the drawer.

discretion (dis-KRESH-un): the ability or right to make decisions independently; also, the ability to be tactful and act with decorum.

Tim's use of profanity at the dinner party showed a startling lack of DISCRETION.

discursive (dis-KUR-siv): rambling; not to the point.

Unfortunately, the study group tended toward long, DISCURSIVE examinations of the day's social events rather than preparation for our term papers.

dishevel (dih-SHEV-ul): to put (hair or clothing) into disarray.

> *Although Adam answered the interview questions intelligently, his DISHEVELED appearance led the interviewer to doubt his professionalism.*

disingenuous (diss-in-JEN-yoo-uss): not inclined toward open dealing; less than truthful; other than appearances would suggest.

> *The Mayor's carefully worded denials never explicitly touched on her involvement in her campaign's alleged effort to buy votes, leading many to conclude that she was being DISINGENUOUS.*

dispel (dis-PELL): to disperse; to drive away.

> *After the rioters had been DISPELLED and the fires put out, an eerie quiet fell over the smoldering city streets.*

dissemble (diss-SEM-bul): to act with an insincere or disguised motive.

> *Although many on the committee were convinced that the undersecretary was DISSEMBLING about how much he knew of rebel activities, there was no hard proof to support this view.*

District of Columbia (DISS-trikt uv kuh-LUM-bee-uh): the capital of the United States; Washington, D.C..

> *The White House, the Congress, and the Supreme Court are located in the DISTRICT OF COLUMBIA.*

diuretic (die-er-ET-ik): tending to increase urination; a drug that causes this increase.

> *After being admitted to the clinic for anorexia, Danielle told the doctors how she had used amphetamines and DIURETICS to speed her weight loss.*

divulge (dih-VULGE): to make known; to reveal or disclose, particularly something that had been secret.

> *The kidnappers refused to DIVULGE the whereabouts of their captive until supplied with safe passage out of the country.*

doctrinaire (dok-trin-AIR): favoring doctrines without concern for their practicability.

> *The resident is not well served by such DOCTRINAIRE advisers as Hawkins.*

doldrums (DOLE-drums): a spell of low feeling; an instance of sadness or stagnation. Also: a specific belt of calms and light winds in the Atlantic and Pacific oceans, difficult to navigate by sail.

> *Kyle is in the DOLDRUMS because he doesn't have enough money to go to the concert with his buddies.*

domain (do-MANE): an area over which one rules; a field within which one has power, influence or authority; a sphere of influence.

> *The local hockey rink was truly Jon's DOMAIN; when he steeped onto the ice, every other player stopped for a moment to watch him with mingled fear and respect.*

double-entendre (DUH-bul on-TON-druh): a statement in which one or many of the words may be interpreted in several ways, resulting in ambiguity; an expression that can be taken two ways, one of which often has sexual or threatening undertones.

> *Although Japanese adult comic books must abide by some very stringent codes forbidding profanity and the overt depiction of sexual activity, they often feature a barrage of steamy DOUBLE-ENTENDRES.*

dour (dowr): grim, stern, or sullen.

> *Nelson, the McKays' DOUR old butler, always made me feel as though I had transgressed some grave social precept in coming to visit Marjorie.*

douse (dowce): to cover with a liquid thoroughly; to drench or soak. (See, for comparison, the entry for *dowse*.)

> *Even after DOUSING the charcoal with lighter fluid, Uncle Al couldn't seem to get the grill fired up.*

downside (DOWN-side): a negative aspect attending a proposal or option; particularly, the potential hazard accompanying a business proposition.

> *The advantage of accepting your proposal, of course, is that it allows us to get the planes back in the air; the DOWNSIDE is that we must accept the decision of the arbitrator as final even if it goes against the interests of our stockholders.*

dowse (dowze): to search for water with a divining rod. (See, for comparison, the entry for *douse*.)

> *A skeptical man by nature, my father refused to believe that we had succeeded in locating the right spot for our well by DOWSING.*

doxology (doks-AH-lo-jee): a hymn praising God.

> *This morning's ceremony will conclude with the DOXOLOGY found on page 312 of your hymnals.*

dregs: literally, the (sediment-bearing) contents of the bottom of a nearly empty container of wine, coffee, or the like; also, something or someone perceived as worthless or as the last and least appealing in a series of choices.

> *Though many in her town looked on ex-convicts as the DREGS of society, it was Debbie's job as a social worker to try to rehabilitate everyone who came through her door, regardless of past history.*

dromedary (DROM-uh-dare-ee): a camel of North Africa and Arabia possessing only one hump.

> *For a small zoo such as ours to have a pair of DROMEDARIES is, I think, something of a coup.*

dross (dross): useless material; trash.

> *The young poet was scarred for life when her father described her poems as "DROSS" and told her to threw them away.*

dupe (doop): to fool, trick, or deceive. As a noun: a person so deceived.

> *Cliff's attempts to DUPE me into finishing his homework for him were about what I expected from an older brother used to getting his own way.*

duplicity (doo-PLISS-ih-tee): trickery; two-facedness; purposeful deceptiveness.

> *Officer Wilkins began to suspect his informant of DUPLICITY, and wondered whether she was leading him into a trap.*

duress (dur-ESS): compulsion resulting from the threat of force; coercion. Also: physical restraint or imprisonment.

> *The prisoner's confession, which had clearly been obtained under DURESS, was instantly ruled inadmissible by the judge.*

dwindle (DWIN-dul): to become smaller; to shrink or waste away; to decrease.

> *I had planned to run away forever, but my DWINDLING supply of cookies and pennies forced me to return home by nightfall.*

ebonite (EBB-ah-nite): hard black rubber; vulcanite.

> *The sturdy EBONITE hoses, flimsy and prone to breakdown in last year's model, were just one of the improvements the company made in its product line.*

ebullition (ebb-uh-LISH-un): the tiny bubbles of a sparkling liquid; also, a sudden outpouring of strong emotion.

> *The champagne's delicate EBULLITION tickled my nose.*

eczema (EG-zuh-muh): an inflammatory skin condition, characterized by red, itching skin that erupts into lesions that later become scaly, hard, and crusty.

> *The skin cleanser Noxzema was named after its supposed ability to "knock ECZEMA."*

eddy (EDD-ee): a small current of air or water that flows against the main current; a small whirlpool or whirlwind.

> *Because it had a strong undertow and a multitude of unpredictable EDDIES, the sound was considered dangerous for even the strongest and most experienced swimmers.*

edifice (ED-ih-fiss): a building, particularly one that is large and imposing.

> *Jacob, who had worked for twelve years in a small family-owned firm, was unprepared for the prospect of working at the Webster corporate headquarters, a massive EDIFICE of brick and glass located in midtown Manhattan.*

efface (ih-FACE): to rub away.

> *Although the letter had been filed and held and folded so many times that the embossed seal pressed into it by the county clerk was nearly EFFACED, it was genuine.*

effect (ih-FECT): a thing taking place as the result of a cause. Also, as a verb (often pronounced ee-FEKT): to cause or influence (a change); to bring about a hoped-for outcome. (See, for comparison, the entry for *affect.*)

> *The entrepreneur's entry into the race had the EFFECT of splitting the Republican vote.*

effervescent (eff-ur-VESS-unt): bubbly; sparkling; lively.

> *Myra's EFFERVESCENT personality makes her a favorite guest at our parties.*

efficacious (eff-ih-KAY-shuss): producing the desired outcome; effective.

> *Tom's lawyer tried a battery of shrewd negotiating techniques during the meeting, but only outright threats to walk away from the deal proved EFFICACIOUS.*

effusion (ih-FYOO-zhun): an outpouring; also, an unrehearsed flow of speech or writing that is emotional in nature.

> *Reviewing the old love letters he had written to Susan, Brian found it hard to believe that the EFFUSIONS of lovestruck prose he found on every page had actually come from his pen.*

e.g. (ee jee): an abbreviation for the Latin term *exempli gratia*, "for example."

> *Many of the luxury cars so popular twenty years ago, E.G., Cadillacs and Lincoln Continentals, have been forced to develop smaller models to compete with today's popular compact vehicles.*

egress (EE-gress): exit.

> *The stewardess's earnest request that we try to make an orderly EGRESS from the burning plane had little effect.*

elapse (ee-LAPS): to pass or go by (said of time).

> *Two hours ELAPSED at the dentist's office before my name was finally called.*

electrolysis (ih-lek-TRAHL-uh-sis) : a process by which unwanted body hair is removed by means of an electric current.

> *Tired of painfully plucking her eyebrows every few days, Judy decided to ask her doctor about ELECTROLYSIS.*

elegy (ELL-uh-jee): a poem of mourning; a poem reflecting on and praising the deceased.

> *At the funeral, Mitch read a touching ELEGY for his grandmother, reminding all present of the life of kindness and sacrifice she had led.*

elixir (e-LIX-ur): a solution meant to be used for medicinal purposes; in medieval times, a supposedly curative drink made from mixing alcohol and drugs in water.

Dr. Callahan's ELIXIR of Life, a patent medicine popular in Kansas in the late 1880s, may have owed part of its popularity to the coca leaves used in its preparation.

emaciated (ee-MAY-shee-ay-tud): dangerously thin.

Winston knew that not everyone would be willing to watch the footage he had shot of the EMACIATED bodies of the famine victims.

emasculate (ee-MASS-kyoo-late): to castrate; also, to deprive of strength or essential elements.

In the editor's view my book had been subject to "deft pruning of occasional offensive passages"; in mine, it had been utterly EMASCULATED.

embezzle (im-BEZ-ul): to appropriate funds for oneself that were placed in one's care for another party.

Bill had always seemed to be a model employee, so the news that he had been EMBEZZLING money from the company for some years came as a complete shock to us all.

emend (ee-MEND): to change by means of editing; to correct (a text or reading). (See, for comparison, the entry for *amend*.)

Many of Shakespeare's most famous lines, such as "A rose by any other name would smell as sweet," are the result of a critic's choice to EMEND a troublesome source text.

emigrant (EM-ih-grunt): one who leaves a country or region for the purpose of settling in another.

The Irish potato famine of the 1840s turned many relatively prosperous citizens into penniless EMIGRANTS bound for the United States.

eminent (EM-ih-nunt): prominent or noted; of high esteem; outstanding and distinguished.

> *I found the prospect of studying physics under an EMINENT professor like Dr. Maxwell, who had just won a Nobel prize, daunting to say the least.*

enclave (ON-klayv):a small territory surrounded by a larger (and usually foreign) one; also, any secluded area.

> *The garden, filled with fragrant flowers and a small, babbling fountain, was an ENCLAVE of serenity in the midst of the busy city.*

encomium (en-KOME-ee-um): a formal (and often, a spoken) expression of extreme praise.

> *The evening, featuring warm ENCOMIUMS for basketball great Larry Bird from coaches, former opponents, and family members, concluded when his jersey was raised to the rafters and his number retired.*

encore (ON-kore): sustained applause, cheers and the like meant to encourage a performer or performers to appear again after the formal conclusion of a performance.

> *It didn't seem possible that the maestro could ignore the our emphatic demands for an ENCORE, but when the houselights went up we all began to file slowly out of the auditorium.*

endeavor (in-DEV-ur): to strive for or attempt; to try to reach.

> *For the better part of a decade, Michael had ENDEAVORED to turn his novel into something that would touch the souls of everyone who read it.*

engender (en-JEN-dur): to beget; to cause to exist.

My decision to move east has ENGENDERED a good deal of hostility on my brother's part.

en masse: (on MASS): in a group; together.

The fans rushed EN MASSE to the front of the auditorium.

enrapture (in-RAP-chur): to delight; to thrill or give pleasure to.

The music of the symphony seemed to ENRAPTURE Olivia, who sat breathless and wide-eyed throughout the performance.

ensemble (on-SOMB-ul): a group of individuals performing together as, for example, a cast of actors or musicians; also, an outfit composed of complementary clothing and accessories.

Mort's time with the jazz ENSEMBLE was humbling after his long career as a solo star, but it was the best musical experience he'd ever had.

ensue (in-SOO): to come afterward; to follow; to happen as a result.

When a tractor-trailer skidded out of control and spilled its load of lumber across Route 128 yesterday afternoon, a huge rush-hour backup ENSUED.

entice (in-TICE): to tempt in a pleasing fashion; to attract or lure.

The delicious aroma emanating from the bakeshop often ENTICES me to stop in and pick up a doughnut or muffin on my way to work.

entomology (en-tuh-MOL-uh-jee): the study of insects.

Judy's little boy so loved to collect bugs from the garden that we wondered if he might grow up to study ENTOMOLOGY.

entourage (ON-too-rahj): a group of associates; people who commonly surround, protect, and attend to someone of importance.

Melanie had hoped to score a front-page story by interviewing the reclusive movie star, but she never made it past his ENTOURAGE.

eon (EE-on): a very long, indefinite period of time; seemingly forever; a span of time beyond comprehension. (In the disciplines of geometry and astronomy, however, eons have specific durations.)

After what felt like several EONS, the tow truck finally arrived and we were able to haul our car back to the campground.

epaulet (EP-uh-let): an ornamental shoulder piece worn on a military uniform.

Ernie tried his best to sew the EPAULET back on his uniform before morning inspection.

ephemeral (ih-FEMM-uh-rul): lasting only a short while.

Our school's joy at winning the state basketball championship turned out to be EPHEMERAL, as the title was suspended when officials learned of the presence of an ineligible player on the team's roster.

epic (EP-ik): of major proportions; extraordinary.

Rosa Park's refusal to go to the back of the bus would take on legendary status in the EPIC struggle for civil rights.

epigram (EP-ih-gram): a short, witty saying or poem.

Alexander Pope was famous for EPIGRAMS, but his body of work features much more profound efforts, as well.

epigraph (EP-ih-graff): an inscription written on a stone, monument or building; also, a short quotation coming at the beginning of a book or chapter.

The EPIGRAPH carved above the entrance to the college library, "That they may have life and have it abundantly," confused some and inspired others.

epilepsy (EP-ih-lep-see): a condition characterized by seizures and tremblings resulting from abnormal rhythmic impulses in the brain.

Researchers believe that many of the "demonic possessions" recounted in the Bible were actually instances of EPILEPSY.

episodic (ep-ih-SOD-ik): made up of episodes; consisting of a group of separate but only externally related anecdotes; tending to digress.

Although the novels of Dickens and Twain still enthrall modern readers, many are puzzled by their EPISODIC structures.

epithet (EP-ih-thet):a word, description or expression (often disparaging) meant to characterize a person.

The EPITHETS used by members of the Nixon administration to describe their political enemies were often unsuitable for publication in family newspapers.

epitome (ee-PIT-uh-mee): the highest or supreme example.

Many people consider "The Mary Tyler Moore Show" to be the EPITOME of 1970s situation comedy.

epoch (EP-uk): a particular time or era notable or significant in history.

> *The first Apollo lunar landing marked the beginning of a new EPOCH for space travel.*

equable (EK-wuh-bull): without variation. (See, for comparison, the entry for *equitable*.)

> *The island boasted a pleasant and EQUABLE climate, with temperatures in the low seventies virtually every day.*

equinox (EK-wih-nox): the point in time when the sun crosses the equator, causing night and day to be of roughly equal length everywhere on earth.

> *The vernal (or spring) EQUINOX generally occurs around March 21; the autumnal equinox, around September 22.*

equitable (EK-wih-tuh-bull): free from bias; just to all involved. (See, for comparison, the entry for *equable*.)

> *The parties have reached what both sides believe to be an EQUITABLE settlement.*

erroneous (ih-RONE-ee-us): wrong.

> *Your suggestion that I spent the summer on the coast of California avoiding writing my book is completely ERRONEOUS.*

erstwhile (URST-hwile): former; of or pertaining to a long-past time.

> *Boston Red Sox fans can only dream of what might have been had their ERSTWHILE star Babe Ruth not been sold to their archrivals, the New York Yankees.*

eschew (ess-CHOO): to shun; to stay away from, especially as a result of moral or ethical concerns.

> *Chuck ESCHEWED his coworkers' nights out on the town, knowing they almost always concluded with a visit to a strip club.*

esplanade (ESS-pluh-nahd): an open, level strip of ground, usually near a body of water.

> *While strolling along the ESPLANADE, we watched the rowing teams train for the upcoming regatta.*

espresso (es-PRESS-oh): a potent, dark coffee brewed by means of forced steam.

> *The ESPRESSO machine had to be one of the most useless birthday presents I'd ever received, given my caffeine intolerance.*

estuary (ESS-choo-ayre-ee): the point of a water passage where a river empties into a tidal area.

> *Dr. Green argued against allowing the plant to be built so near the river, on the grounds that it would threaten several important species living in the ESTUARY.*

et al. (et al): the abbreviation for the Latin term *et alia*, meaning "and others."

> *Members of Congress, the justices of the Supreme Court, the Joint Chiefs of Staff, ET AL. waited for President Clinton to enter and give his first State of the Union address.*

etching (ETCH-ing): an impression on metal or glass made by means of corrosive acid; a picture or design produced by using this process to impart a design on a plate with acid.

> *The ornate images on our paper currency are the result of intricate ETCHINGS meant to foil counterfeiters.*

ethereal (uh-THEER-ee-ul): airy; light; more heavenly than earthly.

> *Norman's paintings had an ETHEREAL quality that gave Lynne an instant sense of peace.*

ethnocentricity (eth-no-sen-TRISS-ih-tee): the belief that cultures different from one's own are inherently inferior.

> *The Nazis displayed a monstrous ETHNOCENTRICITY, to be sure, but they were also pragmatic enough to know when an alliance with the Japanese served their interests.*

euphemism (YOU-fuh-miz-um): a word or expression used as a substitute for one that may be considered offensive or distasteful.

> *My Aunt Polly's quaint EUPHEMISM for "toilet" was "freshening-up room."*

euphonious (you-PHONE-ee-uss); pleasing to the ear.

> *The low, EUPHONIOUS thrumming of the crickets outside my window those summer nights always put me to sleep quickly.*

evade (ee-VADE): to sidestep or dodge; to flee from (a pursuer). (See, for comparison, the entry for *avoid*.)

> *The fugitives EVADED the authorities for three months, but were finally apprehended near Scottsdale, Arizona.*

exalted (ig-ZALT): glorified or praised; held up high in honor.

> *Colvin's album earned the kind of EXALTED commendations usually reserved for major new works of literature.*

excelsior (ik-SEL-see-ur): wood shavings used as a packing agent.

The fragile china was shipped in sturdy wooden crates filled with EXCELSIOR.

except (ek-SEPT); to exclude; also, to express opposition or disagreement to by means of argument. (See, for comparison, the listing for *accept*)

I want everyone we know to come to the dinner party, my old boyfriend EXCEPTED.

excerpt (EK-surpt): to quote or reproduce a portion of a book, play, poem, etc.

Although it may not have been his intention, the rock singer was helping to educate his young audience by using EXCERPTS from the sonnets of Shakespeare in his lyrics.

execrable (ig-ZEK-ruh-bul): disgusting; detestable; vulgar.

Collectors of unauthorized Beatles records must be prepared to pay high prices for the illegal discs, which often feature tracks of EXECRABLE recording quality.

exert (ig-ZURT): to expend effort.

"Please don't EXERT yourself," Alice sneered sarcastically to her husband Fred as he lay on the couch while she vacuumed.

exhilarated (ig-ZILL-uh-rate-ud): to make lively; to excite or energize.

Those evening runs in the cool air of the spring were always EXHILARATING, especially after a day spent cooped up in a stuffy office.

exhort (ig-ZORT): to urge or entreat; to plead with (usually in an attempt to warn or advise).

> *The hostages EXHORTED their captors to give up, arguing that the authorities would deal more leniently with them if no one were hurt.*

exiguous (ex-IG-you-uss): meager; small; scanty.

> *Dinner turned out to be an EXIGUOUS offering of two thin slices of chicken, three green beans, and a potato—albeit quite artistically arranged.*

exodus (EX-uh-duss): a going out; a departure, particularly of a large group of people.

> *After the film reel jammed for the third time, there was a mass EXODUS of angry patrons.*

exonerate (ig-ZON-uh-rate): to clear or free from blame or guilt; to restore (one's reputation).

> *After the charges were thrown out and Brian was completely EXONERATED, he was free to continue his work in the securities industry.*

exorbitant (egg-ZORE-bih-tunt): beyond what is reasonable; extreme or excessive.

> *Christopher had thought he needed a laptop computer to make his business trips easier, but after seeing the EXORBITANT prices, he decided he could go without for another year.*

expedite (EKS-puh-dite): to speed up (a process or action); to complete promptly.

> *My father's friend at the Registry of Motor Vehicles was able to EXPEDITE my driver's license application, and I was spared the standard six-week wait.*

explicit (ik-SPLISS-it): detailed; revealing in full expression; emphatically stated.

> *I felt that certain EXPLICIT scenes in* Last Tango in Paris *were not quite right for five-year-olds, and urged the twins to select a Barney videocassette instead.*

expressionism (ex-PRESH-un-iz-um): an art movement with roots in the late nineteenth and early twentieth centuries in which external forms of reality are distorted as a means of communicating an interior vision of the artist.

> *For Edvard Munch, whose painting* The Scream *is perhaps the single most recognizable image of EXPRESSIONISM, the themes of isolation and anxiety were of paramount importance.*

expunge (iks-PUNGE): to obliterate, remove, or mark for deletion.

> *In exchange for her testimony against her former lover, the charges against Carrie were dropped and her record EXPUNGED of any connection to his crimes.*

expurgate (EX-pur-gate): to remove or delete something unacceptable or objectionable, (particularly, passages in a text).

> *Fearing a public backlash, the publisher promised that all offensive material would be EXPURGATED from future editions of the book.*

extant (ik-STANT): existing; in existence.

> *The EXTANT laws on the subject did not make adequate provisions for issues of sexual harassment, Maria argued, and would have to be updated.*

extempore (iks-TEM-puh-ray): without forethought or preparation; spontaneous, impromptu.

> *As he watched the notecards to his speech fly away in the breeze, Griswold stood before the crowd and wished, once again and more fervently than ever before, that he had the ability to deliver a magnificent speech EXTEMPORE.*

extol (ex-TOLE): to praise highly.

> *The principal EXTOLLED the hard work of the members of the honor society, detailing their many academic achievements for the assembly.*

extradition (eks-tra-DISH-un): the handing over of an alleged fugitive from one country, state, etc., to another.

> *Because there was no formal EXTRADITION agreement between the two countries, the trial of the accused did not begin until two years after the warrant for his arrest had been issued.*

extraneous (ex-TRAY-nee-uss): coming from the outside; not innate; foreign.

> *Miles was a resourceful debater who deflected attacks from his opponents by raising EXTRANEOUS but inflammatory issues.*

extricate (EKS-trih-kate): to remove from an entanglement.

> *Having gotten us into an impossible dilemma, Warren appeared to have no idea how we should go about EXTRICATING ourselves from it.*

extrinsic (iks-TRINZ-ik): not part of the true nature of something.

> *The revolution was less of a spontaneous eruption of anger against capitalism as a system, and more of a reaction to EXTRINSIC forces like the constant oil shortages that came about because of international sanctions.*

exult (ig-ZULT): to celebrate or rejoice heartily.

There was no EXULTING among the families of the victims, who greeted the verdict with a sense of solemn resolution.

facade (fuh-SOD): the ornamental front of a building; also, a false or misleading appearance; a contrived surface meant to deceive.

Not many took the time to look beyond the FACADE of the burly, rough-hewn pig farmer to see the kind-hearted, gentle soul that resided deep inside Big Jim.

facetious (fuh-SEE-shuss): meant to evoke laughter or enjoyment; not intended seriously.

My suggestion that we pack the children off to live with their grandparents for a few decades was FACETIOUS.

facilitate (fuh-SILL-uh-tate): to help, to ease the way.

My knowledge of Moroccan customs FACILITATED our team's negotiations in that country.

facsimile (fak-SIM-uh-lee): an exact copy, imitation, or reproduction.

The centerpiece of Victor's library was a FACSIMILE of the First Folio of the collected plays of Shakespeare.

faction (FAK-shun): a group of persons united within an organization for a common purpose.

The meetings of the board of directors were marked by perpetual squabbling between its two bitterly antagonistic FACTIONS.

fajita (fuh-HEE-tuh): a soft flat tortilla shell filled with chicken, beef (or both) and assorted vegetables; Spanish in origin.

> *This restaurant is famous for its FAJITAS, but I prefer the chimichangas myself.*

falafel (fuh-LOFF-ul): fried food balls or patties consisting of spicy ground vegetables, such as fava beans or chick peas, originating in the Middle East.

> *Moody's in Central Square offers a delicious Middle Eastern dinner special, featuring FALAFEL and lentil soup, for under $5.00.*

fallacy (FALL-uh-see): a misconception; an erroneous perception; a deceit.

> *For some childhood is a time of innocence; but it's a FALLACY to say it is like this for all children.*

fallow (FAL-low); (describing land): uncultivated; plowed but not seeded for a season or more in order to improve the soil. Also: not active or in use.

> *Brenda's creative forces have lain FALLOW since she completed that third novel of hers.*

falsetto (fal-SET-oh): a male singing voice higher than the normal range for that voice. Also: a person who sings falsetto.

> *Our soprano is home with the flu, so poor old Mike is going to have to sing FALSETTO.*

falter (FALL-tur): to hesitate, stumble, or waver; to move uncertainly.

> *Stan had FALTERED so many times in his attempts to ask Julie for a date that his friends began to wonder whether he had ever contemplated simply giving up and becoming a monk.*

farce (farce): a comedy in which situation, satire and preposterous coincidence are predominant over character; also, a ridiculous, empty display not worth serious consideration; a mockery.

> *Although the proceedings were presented to the outside world as a fair trial, Roland knew that he was watching a FARCE in which all the principle witnesses had been bribed to help convict the defendant.*

farrago (fuh-ROG-oh): a careless mixture; mish-mash.

> *My four-year-old, who picked out his own outfit for the first time this morning, walked into the kitchen sporting a FARRAGO of mismatched clothing.*

fauna (FAW-nuh): the animal population of a particular region or time period. (A plural noun.)

> *According to this article, the FAUNA of Australia include more marsupials than are found on any other continent.*

faux (foe): fake or counterfeit in nature.

> *Jill made such commotion over the FAUX pearls I gave her that I began to suspect she thought they were real.*

faze (faze): to bother; to disturb or annoy.

> *We thought Seth would be angry when he found out Phillip was dating his old girlfriend, but the news didn't seem to FAZE him a bit.*

fecund (FEE-kund): fruitful or fertile; prolific.

> *Although he certainly had a FECUND imagination, the screenwriter's most successful efforts had been adaptations of the works of others.*

feign (FANE): to fake or counterfeit; to pretend.

> *Instinctively I knew the man was going to grab for my purse, but I thwarted his efforts by FEIGNING a heart attack, attracting the crowd's attention.*

feint (faint): A false advance or attack intended to catch an opponent off guard.

> *Jim FEINTED several times with his left before decking his opponent with a fierce right cross.*

felicitious (fuh-LISS-uh-tuss): appropriate to the moment or occasion; also, giving great pleasure.

> *Mr. Scott's FELICITIOUS donation to the cause boosted morale among the workers in our tiny soup kitchen.*

felonious (fuh-LONE-ee-uss): criminal; villainous; reminiscent of or relating to a felony crime.

> *Although no court in the land would consider it FELONIOUS, my brother's attempt to blackmail me over that little dent I put in my parent's car was, in my mind, worthy of a long jail sentence.*

femme fatale (femme fuh-TAL): a seductive woman who uses her charms to trick men into compromising or dangerous situations; a woman who uses her feminine wiles for gain.

> *Although the movie industry makes much of its supposed progressiveness, feminists note with disdain that most leading roles for women still lean heavily on stereotype: the ingenue, the FEMME FATALE, the devoted mother battling for her children against all odds.*

femur (FEE-mur): the bone between the pelvis and the knee; the thighbone.

> *The force of the tackle caused a hairline fracture that extended along the entire length of Eli's right FEMUR.*

ferret (FARE-ut): to drive or force out; to discover by forcing out.

> *Colonel Gonzalez declared that he would take any measure necessary to FERRET the rebels out of the hillsides.*

ferrous (FAIR-us): relating to iron; of or pertaining to a substance that contains iron.

> *To counteract the loss of iron during menstruation, many doctors suggest that their female patients take a FERROUS vitamin supplement every day.*

fetters (FET-urz): literally, shackles or handcuffs; a restraint. Also, as a verb (FET-ur): to restrain or restrict movement.

> *The prisoners were led to the bowels of the ship, where narrow wooden benches, FETTERS, and a thin scattering of straw awaited them.*

fibrous (FIE-bruss): made up of fibers; sinewy; of or pertaining to something that can be separated into fibers.

> *With horror I realized that the FIBROUS mass the dog was dragging through the rose bushes was my cashmere sweater—or what was left of it.*

fibula (FIB-you-luh): the large outer bone of the lower portion of the leg.

> *The little brat kicked me so hard I thought for a moment that she might have broken my FIBULA.*

fiefdom (FEEF-dum): the domain over which a feudal lord rules; an area over which one has control or domain.

> *Mr. Duncan treated his wife and children as if they were his subjects, the lucky few privileged to occupy his FIEFDOM.*

filial (FILL-ee-ull): that which is due from or befitting a son or daughter; pertaining to a son a daughter.

> *Mother considered it my FILIAL responsibility to take over the family business when I graduated, but I wanted to pursue a career of my own.*

filibuster (FILL-ih-buss-ter): a legislative tactic by which a member prevents or delays the passage of a law, typically by focusing on irrelevant issues during a long speech to prevent a vote from taking place; any similar technique that monopolizes the floor of legislature by means of parliamentary maneuvers.

> *Even an epic FILIBUSTER staged by Southern legislators could not stop President Johnson from guiding the Civil Rights Act through Congress.*

filigree (FIL-uh-gree): delicate decorative work made of twisted wire.

> *The crown was adorned with beautiful jewels and intricate gold FILIGREE.*

finagle (fih-NAY-gul): to wangle; to use clever, often underhanded methods to achieve one's desires.

> *Justin FINAGLED his way into the press conference by borrowing a pass from another reporter.*

finesse (fih-NESS): using subtle charm and style to resolve a problem; smooth, skillful maneuvering.

> *David's legendary ability to FINESSE his way out of any situation was taxed to the extreme when his wife returned early from a business trip and found him in the hot tub with his secretary.*

finis (fih-NEE): the end or conclusion; also, as an adjective: finished.

> *Many people considered Mr. Clinton's presidential campaign FINIS in the week's before the New Hampshire primary.*

First Amendment (first uh-MEND-munt): an article of the United States Constitution guaranteeing citizens the right to freedom of speech and the free exercise of religion.

> *A court order suppressing this story would be a blatant violation of our newspaper's FIRST AMENDMENT rights.*

fjord (fyord): a thin strip of sea flowing between cliffs or hills.

> *Prison officials were able to determine that the two escapees had managed to escape the island fortress by drugging the guards, crawling through a secret tunnel, and swimming out to the small motorboat accomplices had hidden in the FJORD.*

flaccid (FLASS-id): lacking firmness, stiffness, vigor.

> *After sitting out on the deli counter all day long, the celery stalks and leaves of lettuce looked FLACCID and unappealing.*

flagellate (FLADGE-uh-late): to whip.

> *My daughter, a lifelong animal lover, refused to go on the stage coach ride at the amusement park because of the way the driver FLAGELLATED the horses.*

flak (flak): the bursting shell fired from antiaircraft guns, or an antiaircraft gun itself; also, impediments, arguments, or opposition (to a course of action or situation).

> *"If you give me any more FLAK about the time I set for your curfew," my mom promised, "you won't be going out at all."*

flambé (flom-BAY): to serve in flaming liquor (usually brandy).

> *Although the dinner was only so-so, the raspberry custard FLAMBÉ, which the waiter ignited at our table, was both dramatic and delicious.*

flashback (FLASH-back): to interject a scene containing events from the past into a chronological series of present-day events; an instance of such a scene.

> *Casablanca's FLASHBACK scenes of the two lovers during their time in Paris give us a sense of the love they shared—and the magnitude of Rick's loss.*

flaxen (FLAK-sun): a pale yellow color.

> *I'm not sure Mel would have admired Renee's FLAXEN hair quite so much if he'd known it was the result of a recent visit to the hair salon.*

flimsy (FLIM-zee): lightweight; cheap; unsturdy; of poor quality.

> *The department store circular advertised an amazing sale on bureaus, desks, and other furniture, but when we got to the store we found that all the items we were interested in were constructed from FLIMSY particleboard, not pine or oak.*

flippant (FLIP-unt): disrespectful or harsh in tone; shallow or frivolous.

> *Mario, still upset about the previous night's quarrel, greeted his wife's cheery "Good morning" with a FLIPPANT "Who says it is?"*

floe (FLOW): a large chunk or sheet of floating ice.

> *The penguins would amuse themselves for hours jumping and sliding off the broad, flat FLOES and careening into the water.*

Florida (FLO-rih-duh): the twenty-seventh state of the United States.

> *The capital of FLORIDA is Tallahassee.*

flotilla (floe-TILL-uh): a fleet of ships, usually military vessels; also, any large group of moving objects.

> *On the appointed evening, a massive FLOTILLA of Allied warships—the largest assembly of naval battle vessels in human history—steamed toward Normandy.*

flotsam (FLOT-sum): the debris from a shipwreck that floats on water or is washed ashore.

> *When they collected and examined the FLOTSAM from the Intrepid, investigators found minute traces of dynamite that proved once and for all that the ship's explosion was not the result of a faulty fuel line.*

flounder (FLOWN-dur): to struggle clumsily. (See, for comparison, the entry for *founder*.) Also: a fish.

> *My FLOUNDERING efforts to open the door while holding five packages were the object of some amusement to my roommate, but he did not offer to relieve me of any of them.*

fluctuate (FLUK-choo-ate): to waver between one thing and another; to change or shift back and forth constantly.

The dietitian said we should not worry if our weight FLUCTUATED between two and five pounds in either direction of our goal, as long as we were able to maintain a weight in that range.

flue (floo): a duct or tube used for the passage of smoke.

David vowed to spend Christmas Eve staring up the FLUE so he could alert the family the moment Santa arrived, but he fell asleep after only a short time at his post.

fluency (FLOO-un-see): ready and unhindered expression.

Alice's FLUENCY in Spanish proved a real advantage during our trip to Mexico.

fob (FOB): to get rid of (usually by unscrupulous means).

Don't let him fool you; those "courtside" tickets he's trying to FOB off on you at such a bargain price are counterfeit.

foliage (FOLE-ee-udge): a group of leaves, branches, and flowers.

The best time to view the fall FOLIAGE in New England is at generally early October, when the reds, oranges, and golden yellows are at their most brilliant.

foment (fo-MENT): to aid, nourish, feed, or encourage.

Some in the university argued that our group's purpose was to FOMENT a revolution, not work for reform, and they demanded that we dissolve.

foolhardy (FOOL-har-dee): rash; hasty; unthinking.

> *Mack's FOOLHARDLY decision to leave his job and visit Trinidad and Tobago for two years was apparently the result of a chance encounter with a palm reader he met in a Greyhound station in West Covina, California.*

forage (FOR-uj): to search or hunt for food and provisions.

> *I awoke just in time to find the dog FORAGING in our picnic basket.*

forcible (FORCE-ih-bul): powerful; using force to achieve a goal.

> *The editors of the campus paper were shocked at the campus police's FORCIBLE entry into their offices.*

forebear (FORE-bare): an ancestor; forefather.

> *Kate's illustrious FOREBEAR was a preeminent figure in the abolitionist movement.*

foreclosure (fore-CLOZH-er): the act of repossessing a mortgaged property due to a default on payments, resulting in the mortgagee losing all rights to the property.

> *Neither Mrs. Walker nor her estranged husband could keep up the mortgage payments on the condo during their divorce proceedings, and the bank FORECLOSED on the property.*

foreordained (fore-or-DANED): to ordain or appoint in advance; predestined.

> *Although Milton viewed his promotion to management as FOREORDAINED, his wife had her doubts.*

forge (forj): to form and mold metals or other materials by using intense heat; to expend effort for the purpose of creating something; to fuse or join two formerly disparate elements.

> *By the end of the rigorous Outward Bound weekend, the friends had FORGED a bond that would last a lifetime.*

forsake (for-SAKE): to abandon.

> *Emily has FORSAKEN California for an island in the Indian Ocean.*

forte (fort): one's niche or strong point; that at which one excels.

> *Interior decorating was Frank's FORTE, but he resisted making a career of it for fear of what "the guys" would say.*

forum (FOR-um): a gathering, meeting, or program held for the purpose of discussing matters of public or common concern.

> *"Although I am sure your neighbor's constantly barking dog is irritating, Mrs. Wakefield," the chairman intoned, "the purpose of this FORUM is to discuss the proposed waste site."*

founder (FOUN-dur): to sink; to fail in an undertaking. (See, for comparison, the entry for *flounder*.)

> *The new firm FOUNDERED because the promised investment capital never materialized.*

four-flusher (FOR-flush-ur): In poker, a player who bluffs.

> *Our Friday-night poker games aren't played with the highest degree of honesty; everyone involved is a well-known FOUR-FLUSHER.*

foyer (FOY-ur): hall; vestibule; entryway; a lobby (as in a theater or hotel).

> *"If the FOYER is any indication of what I'll find on the upper floors," I thought to myself, "my new office is going to be a real dump."*

fracas (FRAK-us): commotion; a noisy disagreement.

> *The nightly FRACAS between the couple next door is always loud enough to wake me out of a sound sleep.*

fraught (frot): loaded or filled with; accompanied by; involving.

> *Buck accepted the task, although he knew it was FRAUGHT with peril.*

frenetic (fruh-NET-ik): frantic; frenzied.

> *I tried to avoid the FRENETIC Christmas rush by buying presents over the summer.*

frenzy (FREN-zee): a state of wild excitement; extreme emotional or mental agitation.

> *What with studying for the bar exam and planning her wedding, Sara had been in an almost constant FRENZY for nearly two months.*

frisson (free-SON): a brief shudder of excitement; a thrill.

> *Maria felt a FRISSON of joy at winning the drama award, but it was tempered by the fact that one of the people she had beaten out was her best friend.*

froufrou (FROO-froo): excessive or unnecessary decoration; especially, an elaborate adornment in women's fashion.

> *Angela had never seen so many ill-fitting tuxedoes and self-conscious frills and FROUFROUS than she beheld the night of the senior prom.*

frowzy (FROW-zee): sloppy; unkept; stale.

> *One would never know that beneath those FROWZY, oversized dresses and grungy cowboy hats was a model who had recently appeared on the cover of Vogue.*

fugue (fyoog): a piece of music that builds up from a central theme.

> *Many music enthusiasts find Bach's FUGUES more hauntingly beautiful than his sonatas and cantatas.*

fulcrum (FUL-krum): the point of support on which a lever turns.

> *To illustrate the function of a FULCRUM, Mr. Hess directed our attention to the window, where two children could be seen playing on a see-saw in the park.*

fulsome (FUL-sum): excessive and overdone, especially in a way inconsistent with good taste. Also: insincerely earnest in expression.

> *Although Marian greeted my work with FULSOME praise, it was clear to me within five minutes of our meeting that she hadn't read a page of it.*

fumigate (FYOO-mih-gate): to release fumes in order to get rid of insects or other pests.

> *We had the place FUMIGATED, used sound-waves, and set dozens of traps, but our house continued to be plagued by cockroaches.*

furbelow (FUR-buh-low): a showy ruffle.

> *Deborah's floor-length dress ended in a beautiful silk FURBELOW.*

furlough (FUR-low): a leave of absence, especially for a member of the armed forces; the act of granting this leave.

> *During his FURLOUGH Dan concentrated on finding a job in the private sector, as he was scheduled to be discharged from the Navy in three months.*

furor (FYOOR-ur): widespread excitement or anger; fury or uproar among persons or institutions.

> *Governor White's indictment for embezzlement caused a FUROR in the state.*

futurism (FYOO-chur-ih-zim): an early 20th-century arts movement stressing the dynamics and movements of the industrial age.

> *Jones was fascinated by early industrial art; last semester he took a course on FUTURISM.*

futz (futs): to pass the time idly or without purpose.

> *Kevin spent so much time this morning FUTZING around with his new espresso maker that he was late for work.*

gadabout (GAD-uh-bout): a person who wanders about aimlessly or restlessly, especially one in constant search of pleasure.

> *Though most everyone thought of her as a flighty GADABOUT, Karen certainly knew when to bear down and get serious about her schoolwork.*

gadfly (GAD-fly): a fly that bites livestock; also, one who annoys, irritates or provokes.

> *With his constant grumbling and irritating habits, Morton has turned into the GADFLY of our department.*

galore (guh-LORE): in abundance; plentiful.

> *Once Mom hit the lottery, she promised, it would be presents GALORE for all of us: new cars, clothes, jewelry, vacations, and just about anything else we wanted.*

galvanize (GAL-vuh-nize): to stimulate into action; to motivate (as if with an electric shock).

> *After considerable national debate over the merits of entering into a "European war," the Japanese attack on Pearl Harbor GALVANIZED American public opinion as nothing else could.*

gambit (GAM-but): in chess, an opening in which a piece is sacrificed with the hope of gaining strategic advantage; also, any maneuver or plan calculated to gain advantage.

> *Bill's plan to get the inside track on the new position by dating the boss's daughter was a risky and ill-conceived GAMBIT that ended in failure.*

gamesome (GAIM-sum): merry; frolicsome.

> *It's sad to see that Sally has become such a stick-in-the mud; as a young woman, she was so GAMESOME and full of high spirits.*

gamin (GAM-in): an urchin; a youngster who lives in the streets.

> *Much of the material for Dickens' Oliver Twist—the intolerable conditions of the orphanage, the streetwise GAMINS, the reprehensible exploiters of the innocent—came from Dickens' own early life.*

garret (GARE-ut): an attic room; also, a secluded, generally unfinished area near the top of a structure used as an observation post or as a place for privacy and refuge.

> *Although he had a computer and printer set up in his downstairs study, Christopher found that he did his best writing sitting up in the GARRET with a pad of paper and a pencil.*

gastropod (GAS-tro-pawd): a variety of mollusk having no shell or a single spiral shell and moving by means of a ventral disk or foot.

> *June retorted that she hadn't ever considered eating GASTROPODS in the United States, and saw no reason to do so in France no matter what they were called.*

gaunt (gawnt): extremely thin; haggard, as by deprivation or worry.

> *The televised images of the hostages showed the world a series of GAUNT faces, worn by months of torture and captivity, reading words that had obviously been written for them.*

gazebo (guh-ZEE-boe): a small outdoor structure, roofed but open on the sides, usually placed in a backyard or a park.

> *The GAZEBO in the church courtyard was freshened up with a new coat of white paint every spring in preparation for outdoor weddings.*

gazetteer (gah-zih-TEER): a dictionary or index of geographical locations.

> *The Smiths' method of deciding where to go on their vacation is to open the GAZETTEER at random and stab the page with a finger; whatever they land on will become their summer destination.*

gemology (jeh-MALL-uh-jee): the study of gems.

> *Despite a lifelong interest in GEMOLOGY, Lucas knew he was in no position to make a valid assessment of the stone's worth.*

gendarme (zhon-DARM): an officer in a police force in any of several European countries, but particularly those of France.

> *After months of difficult undercover work, the Parisian GENDARME was able to recover the stolen artwork and return it to its rightful place in the Louvre.*

generic (juh-NARE-ik): of or pertaining to all members of a group or category; also, unprotected by trademark; common and unremarkable.

> *Senator Smith used the press conference as an opportunity to deliver his GENERIC speech on the role of the media in the development of public policy.*

genre (ZHAWN-ruh): a particular style that characterizes a type of music, art, literature, film, etc.

> *Though their GENRE doesn't make for pleasant or easy reading, one has to admire muckrakers like Upton Sinclair, who aimed to bring about important social reforms with their novels.*

Georgia (JYORJ-uh): the fourth state of the United States.

> *The capital of GEORGIA is Atlanta.*

germane (jur-MAYN): pertinent; relevant; related to the matter at hand.

> *The defendant's exemplary qualities as a breadwinner are hardly GERMANE to the question of whether he shot his cousin, Your Honor.*

gerontocracy (jare-un-TOCK-ruh-see): a group in which the order and rule is kept by a group of elders; government by the older members of a society.

One of the potential drawbacks of a GERONTOCRACY, of course, is that people entrusted with great political power may well become mentally infirm.

gerontology (jare-un-TOL-uh-jee): the field of medicine concerned with illnesses, diseases, and problems specific to old age.

My decision to enter the field of GERONTOLOGY was greeted with skepticism by my father, who had hoped I would follow in his footsteps and become a general practitioner.

gerrymander (JARE-ee-man-dur): to divide voting districts in such a way as to give unfair advantage to a particular party.

Senator Belger dismissed the charges of racist GERRYMANDERING that had been made against him as so much hogwash from opponents eager to draw the district maps to their own liking.

gibber (JIB-bur): to speak nervously and incomprehensibly; to speak in a fast, jumbled, inarticulate manner.

Zack may have been believable playing the part of a Casanova in the television show, but off-screen he could barely GIBBER his way through a conversation with a woman.

gild (gild): to cover thinly with gold; also, to make something appear more valuable or appealing than it actually is.

> *Ross attempted to GILD his offer by promising not to lay off current employees for at least two years, but the board's only question was whether he could match the $630 million figure put forth by the Stradbury group.*

gimcrackery (JIM-crack-ur-ee): an object or objects that has no real value except for the purpose of show.

> *Paul's father used to tell him that all the academic honors he earned in college amounted to so much GIMCRACKERY if he couldn't put his intelligence to work for him in the "real" world.*

gingivitis (jin-jih-VIE-tuss): a gum disease; the condition of having swollen gums.

> *The rinse promised lifetime protection against GINGIVITIS, a claim Fred viewed with some skepticism.*

gist (jist): the main point; the essential meaning, the core or heart of a message.

> *The GIST of the letter from the grievance committee is that the workers are tired of being unappreciated and underpaid.*

glaucoma (glaw-KOE-muh): a disease of the eye caused by increasing pressure on the eyeball, creating damage to the optic disk that, if severe enough, can cause loss of vision.

> *The portion of my annual visit to the eye doctor that I like the least is the GLAUCOMA test, in which a blast of air is shot into each eye at close range.*

glean (gleen): to collect; to gain bit by bit; to obtain one piece or morsel at a time.

> *Although Mr. Willis never came out and said as much, his secretary was able to GLEAN that he would soon be retiring.*

glib (glib): articulate yet superficial; facile.

> *I asked for an analysis of the construction of Shakespeare's tragedies, but you have turned in a series of GLIB observations on the most famous speeches in the plays.*

glissade (glih-SOD): in mountain climbing, a slide down a steep, snow-covered slope.

> *The instructor had made the GLISSADE look easy, but as I looked after him down the slope, I had a feeling my own trek down wouldn't be quite as smooth.*

glissando: (glih-SAHN-doe): in music, a smooth transition between intervals, such as the sound a slide trombone or pedal steel guitar makes in moving from one note to another.

> *Since there is no way to "bend" its notes, the piano cannot produce a true GLISSANDO.*

glower (GLOU-ur): to give a brooding, annoyed, or angry look.

> *Mark hoped GLOWERING at our mother would convey that he didn't appreciate her telling his new girlfriend how difficult he had been to toilet train, but Mom didn't seem to notice.*

gnash (nash): to grind or strike (usually the teeth) together.

> *Although she claimed not to be, I could tell that Elaine was angry by the way she GNASHED her teeth.*

gnocchi (NYAW-kee): an Italian pasta dish; small round balls of pasta.

> *Dawn ordered GNOCCHI for Ellen, her five-year-old, but the little girl seemed to enjoy playing with the little things more than eating them.*

gossamer (GOSS-uh-mer): a delicate, floating film of cobwebs; also: thin and light, and therefore reminiscent of gossamer.

> *Some mornings, the grass outside our house takes on a veil of GOSSAMERS.*

goulash (GOO-losh): a stew made with beef, vegetables, and paprika.

> *The chef's famous GOULASH was an old family recipe that had been handed by from his Hungarian ancestors for generations.*

gourmand (GOOR-mahnd): one who eats well and to excess.

> *A well-known GOURMAND, Uncle Abe was forced to change his eating habits after his heart attack.*

grapple (GRAP-ul): to struggle (with an opponent or enemy); to attempt to pin down or throw to the ground.

> *Alert Secret Service agents GRAPPLED with the armed intruder and wrestled him to the ground before any shots were fired.*

gratis (GRAT-iss): free of charge.

> *I liked visiting Renee when she was working at the ice cream parlor, but the sundaes and banana splits she always offered GRATIS were impossible to resist—and they weren't helping my diet much.*

gratuity (gruh-TOO-ih-tee): a tip; extra money given for service beyond the amount required by the bill.

> *I make it a point never to leave a GRATUITY if the service has been truly horrible.*

grenadine (GREN-uh-deen): reddish-orange in color; also, a pomegranate-flavored syrup used in preparing mixed drinks.

> *Ted had planned to make Tequila Sunrises for the party, but as he had no GRENADINE to add a hint of red, he called the drinks "Tequila Sunbursts."*

grievous (GREE-vuss): grave; severe; causing or likely to cause grief.

> *Failing to get a tune-up before driving to the shore turned out to be a GRIEVOUS error: I broke down in the middle of nowhere and had to pay a small fortune for a tow truck.*

grisly (GRIZ-lee): gruesome.

> *The final confrontation with Brando's character, GRISLY though it is, effectively follows through on the themes of ritual sacrifice established earlier in the film.*

gruel (grool): a thin, soup-like dish made from cooked cereal or grain.

> *In one of the most memorable scenes Dickens ever wrote, young Oliver Twist loses a lottery among the workhouse boys and must ask for an unprecedented second helping of GRUEL.*

guffaw (guh-FAW): an instance of full, unrestrained laughter.

> *From the howls and GUFFAWS I heard issuing from the auditorium, I gathered that the principal's speech introducing a new dress code for the school was not going well.*

guild (gild): a group of people dedicated to common interests or goals; an association of like-minded individuals.

> *Although she knew it was only a first step, Andrea couldn't help feeling that joining the Screen Actors GUILD meant she was on her way to becoming a star.*

guise (guys): semblance; outer appearance; manner of dress.

> *Having assumed the GUISE of a pirate for the costume ball, Tom looked dashing and dangerous for what may well have been the first time in his life.*

gullible (GULL-ih-bull): easily cheated, tricked, or deceived.

> *I'm afraid Terry is a little too GULLIBLE to survive for long as an aspiring actor in a city like New York.*

guru (GOO-roo): an inspiring spiritual or intellectual leader; a revered teacher.

> *Though I found the self-help seminar to be helpful enough, I wasn't as awed as some others in the course, who made the instructor out to be some kind of GURU.*

guttural (GUTT-er-ul): harsh or raspy; reminiscent of deep sounds produced in the throat. Also: of or pertaining to the throat.

> *The dog let out a low, GUTTURAL growl that was likely to give pause to whomever was standing on the other side of the door.*

gyrate (JIE-rate): to spin; to wind or coil.

> *"What you kids do today isn't dancing," said Grandma; "all you do is jump and GYRATE willy-nilly."*

habiliment (huh-BIL-eh-ment): a piece of clothing; a garment.

> *Much to the puzzlement of his staid colleagues, Professor Herriot looked upon the hippies of the 1960s, with their unorthodox choices in lifestyle and HABILIMENT, as welcome additions to a stagnant social order.*

hacienda (ha-see-EN-duh): a large estate or plantation.

> *After spending his junior year living on a HACIENDA while he studied Spanish in Madrid, Oscar had a tough time readjusting to his tiny dorm room.*

haggis (HAG-iss): a dish originating in Scotland made by removing the heart, liver, and lungs of a sheep or cow, dicing these, adding onions, suet, oatmeal, and seasonings, and placing the mixture into the animal's stomach, and boiling it.

> *Ivan had been enjoying the HAGGIS Mrs. MacIntyre had prepared for him until he asked her how it was made.*

haggle (HAG-ul): to bargain with; to dicker or negotiate on price or terms.

> *I think Tom enjoyed the process of HAGGLING at the flea market more than the items he bought.*

hale (hale): healthy and vigorous; disease-free.

> *Lydia had been assured by the surgeon that she'd be HALE and hearty again in two weeks.*

hallucinogenic (huh-loo-sih-noe-JEN-ik): reminiscent of or pertaining to a drug or other substance that causes imaginary visions or delusions.

> *It seems difficult to believe that any person would knowingly administer HALLUCINOGENIC drugs to a seven-year-old child, Your Honor, but such are the facts before us in this case.*

halyard (HAL-yurd): a tackle or rope usually used on ships to help hoist and lower sails.

> *As the storm intensified, Mary told us to slacken the HALYARD while Billy tried to guide the boat back toward shore.*

harangue (huh-RANG): lecture; berate; also, an instance of such berating.

> *Professor Thomas kept me after class to HARANGUE me for handing in a handwritten term paper.*

harbinger (HAR-bin-jur): someone or something that announces the approach of another, or of a forthcoming event.

> *The artist's mediocre early work, while commercially unsuccessful, did serve as a HARBINGER of future triumphs that dealing with similar themes.*

118

harlequin (HAR-luh-kwin): a comic character from the Italian *commedia* tradition, usually masked and wearing a tight-fitting costume.

> *Instead of the standard joker, the ornamental deck of playing cards featured a HARLEQUIN in colorful attire.*

harried (HARE-eed): frazzled or troubled.

> *The HARRIED parents began to despair of keeping track of so many children at the museum.*

harrowing (HARE-roe-ing): extremely distressing; disturbing or frightening in the extreme.

> *After her HARROWING ride down a hill in a car with failed brakes, Monica vowed never to drive again.*

haughty (HAUT-ee): snobbishly proud.

> *I tried to apologize for bumping into the woman, but she only gave me a HAUGHTY glance and inspected her fur coat for damage.*

Hawaii (huh-WIE-ee): the fiftieth state of the United States.

> *The capital of HAWAII is Honolulu.*

hedonist (HEE-duh-nist): one whose life is devoted solely or primarily to the pursuit of pleasure and gratification.

> *I took offense at Jane's implication that a glass of white wine during dinner made some kind of HEDONIST.*

heed (heed): to pay attention to; to take into consideration; as a noun, an instance of notice or attention.

> *Don't pay my brother George any HEED; he always tries to make me look bad in front of my dates.*

heirloom (AIR-loom): a possession of commercial or sentimental value handed down from generation to generation.

> *As the oldest child, I was given the most precious family HEIRLOOM, our old grandfather clock, when my mother passed away.*

heliocentric (hee-lee-oh-SEN-trick): of or pertaining to the theory that the sun is the center of the solar system; having the sun at the center; also, seen as from the center of the sun.

> *At the time Copernicus published his theory that our solar system is HELIOCENTRIC, the orthodox teaching was that the sun and all other planets revolved around the earth.*

helter-skelter (HEL-tur SKEL-tur): haphazard; lacking order or purpose; confused in manner or array.

> *While the children ran HELTER-SKELTER through the living room, Mrs. Moore tried to light the candles on her son's birthday cake and set out party bags.*

hemophilia (hee-mo-FEE-lee-uh): a blood defect usually affecting males but transmitted by females in which the blood fails to clot normally, often leading to uncontrolled hemorrhaging.

> *Because so many HEMOPHILIA patients have contracted the AIDS virus from contaminated blood, many will only accept transfusions using blood that has been donated by family and friends.*

hemorrhoid: a condition where the mass of tissues at the base of the anus becomes swollen as a result of dilated veins.

After enduring a thirty-hour labor and a severe case of post-partum HEMORRHOIDS, Meg doubted she'd ever have another child.

hereditary (huh-RED-ih-tare-ee): passed through the genes from parents to their children.

Although the doctors of his time believed him to be suffering from a host of exotic contagious illnesses, experts now believe that George III's madness was caused by HEREDITARY factors.

heresy (HARE-uh-see): an instance of espousing religious beliefs contrary to a church doctrine.

After having been suppressed centuries ago as HERESY, the newly discovered Gospel of Thomas has given scholars and lay readers valuable insights on the teachings of Jesus.

hermaphrodite (hur-MAFF-ruh-dite): one who possesses both male and female reproductive organs.

Sheldon brought back miniature statues of the island's mythic hero, a HERMAPHRODITE warrior.

hibachi (hih-BOCH-ee): a small, table-top charcoal grill.

The manager of the apartment complex would not allow her tenants to keep full-sized gas or charcoal grills on the balconies, but she did make occasional allowances for HIBACHIS.

highbrow (HIE-brow): intelligent and cultured; also, one who is pretentious or snobby about intelligence and culture.

Al liked going to gallery shows to see the work of new artists, but he found the HIGHBROW analysis of some of his fellow patrons almost unbearable.

highfalutin (hi-fuh-LOO-tin): pompous; pretentious; overblown and extravagant.

> *Al said he'd rather have root canal work than attend another one of Gina's HIGHFALUTIN dinner parties and suffer in humiliation for not using the proper utensils for each course.*

hinterlands (HIN-tur-lands): an area far away from the coastline; also, an area far removed from a city.

> *The blizzard dumped nearly three feet of snow on my relatives in the HINTERLANDS, while those of us in town had to deal with icy rain and flooding.*

hippodrome (HIP-uh-drome): an arena for events such as circuses and horse shows.

> *Once a year Dad would take us down to the HIPPODROME in Springville for the 4-H Club's exposition.*

hirsute (HUR-soot): hairy.

> *"Here you are, my HIRSUTE friend," Dr. Fredericks called out, "a nice juicy bone from the butcher."*

hoarfrost (HORE-frost): white, frozen dew that coats surfaces on winter mornings.

> *A layer of HOARFROST had covered the drab garden in silver, and the children squealed that the frost fairies had come.*

hobgoblin (HOB-gob-lin): a goblin purported to engage in mischievous behavior.

> *Ever since I read her those fairy stories the other night, my daughter has tried to convince me that a HOBGOBLIN is responsible for every piece of mischief she gets into.*

hologram (HOLL-uh-gram): a three-dimensional image created electronically and without a lens.

> *The HOLOGRAM was such a convincing illusion that the dog actually barked at the image of its owner, apparently expecting to be fed.*

homeopathy (ho-mee-OP-uh-thee): a means of treating a disease by administering small doses of medicine that, in large doses, would bring about effects similar to the disease being treated.

> *HOMEOPATHY relies on the body's ability to develop immune responses in warding off disease.*

homiletics (hom-ih-LET-iks): the art of preaching.

> *Rather than risk being swayed by the HOMILETICS of its proponents and opponents, Grandpa made it a point to read the text of every ballot initiative in full before deciding how he would vote on it.*

homily (HOM-uh-lee): a religious talk or speech, usually given to a congregation; a talk that expounds on religious themes.

> *Father Graham's HOMILY on the power of faith inspired Warren to go home and try to work through his problems with his wife.*

homogeneous (ho-mo-JEE-nee-uss): the same throughout; made up of like parts; not heterogeneous.

> *The island supported a small HOMOGENEOUS population of aboriginal tribes.*

hookah (HOOK-uh): a large multistemmed smoking apparatus that cools smoke by passing it through water.

> *Terry brought back many artifacts from her trip to India, including incense, silk saris, and even an antique HOOKAH.*

horde (hord): a large crowd; a swarm of people.

Outside the department store, HORDES of angry shoppers, having been told that the doors would swing open at eight o'clock sharp, began to press against the huge window.

horrific (hor-RIFF-ik): horrifying; scary; terrifying.

Mr. Benton insisted on reading the newspaper's account of the HORRIFIC train wreck out loud during lunch.

hosanna (ho-ZAN-uh): from the Hebrew for "save us"; now an expression of praise, exaltation, and adoration typically heard in religious ceremonies; also, an instance of excessive praise.

Mel's agent warned him not to take too seriously the HOSANNAS that came his way after he won the acting award.

house organ (HOUS-or-gun): a magazine or newsletter published by an organization for distribution within the organization.

I read about Joanne's promotion to sales manager in the last issue of On the Line, *our HOUSE ORGAN.*

hovel (HUV-ul): a modest, humble home or hut; a rude or dirty dwelling-place.

In the storm scenes of King Lear, *Edward is disguised as Poor Tom, a lunatic who has sought shelter in a HOVEL on the barren heath.*

hubbub (HUB-ub): a commotion; an outburst.

The HUBBUB outside our window came as a surprise; the parade was not due for an hour, yet the streets were already thronged with people.

hybrid (HIE-brid): the result of a mixture or combination of two dissimilar things (as in two breeds of animals, or two types of flowers).

Raymond spent all of his free time in the greenhouse perfecting his beautiful HYBRID orchids.

hydraulic (hie-DROLL-ik): related to the study of water, its properties, circulation, and distribution; powered by water.

Senator Graham argued that harnessing the river could provide HYDRAULIC power to three counties.

hypertension (hi-pur-TEN-shun): high blood pressure; the condition that occurs as a result of high blood pressure.

Some over-the-counter cough, cold, and allergy medicines tend to cause elevated blood pressure, and include with a warning that they may be hazardous to those suffering from HYPERTENSION.

hypocrite (HIP-uh-krit): a person pretending to be something he or she is not, or pretending, for the sake of appearance, to have high moral beliefs; a person who does not act according to espoused beliefs.

In Marilyn's view, a marriage counselor who advised others to live up to the ideal of fidelity but who cheated on his own wife was the worst kind of HYPOCRITE.

hypodermic (hi-puh-DUR-mik): related to parts under the skin; made expressly for the purpose of introducing medications via injection.

For Greg the mere sight of a HYPODERMIC needle was enough to produce a panic attack.

hypothesis (hie-POTH-uh-suss): an educated guess; a proposition; an untested theory put forth to explain something.

> *Our task was to test the instructor's HYPOTHESIS that constant exposure to high-pitched sounds impedes the growth of plants.*

ibid. (ih-bid): abbreviation for "ibidem," literally "in the place mentioned before." (The word is typically used in bibliographies and other reference materials to indicate that a quote from a previously referenced source is being repeated.)

> *Mark's overreliance on a single source was evident in the paper's bibliography, which consisted of one reference to Mill's* On Liberty *and seventy-six notations reading "IBID."*

iconoclast (eye-KON-uh-klast): a person who supports the destruction of holy images, or, more broadly, someone who challenges the status quo.

> *The first-year student's repeated verbal attacks on the art department , the president of the university, and the capitalist structure of society earned him a reputation as an ICONOCLAST.*

Idaho (EYE-duh-ho): the forty-third state of the United States.

> *The capital of IDAHO is Boise.*

ideogram (ID-ee-o-gram): a symbol representing an idea rather than a word.

> *For foreigners, the most difficult part of learning to write in Chinese is generally mastering its many IDEOGRAMS.*

idiosyncrasy (ih-dee-oh-SINK-ruh-see): a behavioral quirk or eccentricity.

> *One of my coworkers likes to engage in a brief round of calisthenics at the top of every hour, a harmless-enough IDIOSYNCRASY.*

idle (EYE-dul): not put to use; inactive. Also: lacking in substance. (See, for comparison, the entry for *idol.*)

> *When the phone service went down, our customer service operators had to sit IDLE at their stations, which drove Mr. Brown to distraction.*

idol (EYE-dul): a worshiped image; a figure of a god. Also, any personage who is the object of devotion. (See, for comparison, the entry for *idle.*)

> *That flamenco dancer she went to see last week is my sister Cassandra's latest IDOL.*

idolatry (eye-DOLL-uh-tree): the worship of a physical object as though it were a god or idol; to display an unusual and worshipful attachment to an object.

> *Buddy's IDOLATRY of his shiny new Corvette led a couple of his friends to remark that he would take it to bed with him if he could.*

idyllic (eye-DILL-icky): pleasing; peaceful; ideal.

> *Our IDYLLIC honeymoon in the tropics was interrupted by a tropical hurricane.*

i.e. (eye ee): an abbreviation for the Latin expression *id est,* meaning "that is."

> *Please make sure your child comes to school on the first day with all the necessary supplies, I.E., pencils, erasers, and notebooks.*

ilk (ilk): family, type, or category.

> *I have no use for such vapid writers as Crennenfield, or anyone of his ILK.*

Illinois (ill-ih-NOY): the twenty-first state of the United States.

> *The capital of ILLINOIS is Springfield.*

imbecility (im-buh-SILL-ih-tee): foolishness; simplemindedness.

> *Although he lamented the IMBECILITY of mainstream television, Arnie was not above an occasional viewing of American Gladiators or Geraldo.*

immerse (im-MURCE): to plunge into or surround with liquid.

> *Radios, electric shavers, and other electrical appliances can deliver lethal electric shocks if IMMERSED in water while plugged in.*

imminent (IM-uh-nunt): likely to happen at any time; impending.

> *With his plane's departure IMMINENT, Greg gave his little girl a hug for the last time, kissed her on the forehead, and headed toward the gate.*

impale (im-PALE): to pierce with a sharp object; to pin or hold down.

> *Carol, with her flair for the dramatic, urged her husband to fix the loose pickets on the fence before one of the neighborhood children was IMPALED.*

impecunious (im-pih-KYOO-nee-uss): lacking in money; having little or nothing in the way of funds.

When Greg and Cheryl first met, their IMPECUNIOUS circumstances led them to take a lot of long walks instead of going out to dinner or dancing.

impede (im-PEED): to obstruct progress; to block.

The fire regulations are quite clear on the question of storage in this hallway; nothing is allowed to IMPEDE access to the main exit.

imperiled (im-PARE-uld): endangered.

Fred knew that if he stumbled on the final history test of the year, the B-plus average he had worked toward all semester long would be IMPERILED.

impolitic (im-PAWL-i-tick): not expedient; injudicious.

After a few drinks, Uncle Roland has an unfortunate habit of making IMPOLITIC remarks about my father's failed business ventures.

importune (im-por-TOON): to request repeatedly so as to be a bother.

After months of IMPORTUNING his employer for a promotion that did not yet exist, Hank was asked to leave the company.

imposition (im-puh-ZISH-un): an instance of inconvenience or the laying on of obligation; the act of causing another to take on a burden.

I knew full well that our staying with Aunt Sadie for six months was an IMPOSITION, but while the house was being built we really had no other choice.

impresario (im-pruh-SAHR-ee-o): a person who organizes or sponsors entertainment or cultural events (such as concerts and plays).

> *Quentin's career as an IMPRESARIO came to an abrupt halt when he lost all his investors' money on a musical version of Marx's* Das Kapital.

impressionism (im-PRESH-un-iz-im): an art movement of the late nineteenth century dedicated to reproducing the effect of light on objects, typically by means of short brush strokes.

> *The painter and sculptor Edgar Degas was one of the foremost practitioners of IMPRESSIONISM.*

imprimatur (im-pruh-MAH-ter): approval granted, usually by the Roman Catholic Church, to publish a book.

> *After directing several revisions of the controversial book's text, the Church finally gave its IMPRIMATUR.*

impromptu (im-PRAHMP-too): spontaneous; not planned or rehearsed; conceived on the spur of the moment.

> *Sonya's IMPROMPTU New Year's Eve dinner party ended up being more fun than any of the formal affairs our group of friends had attended for New Years past.*

inadvertent (in-ud-VERT-unt): unintentional; not on purpose; accidentally.

> *I INADVERTENTLY called attention to Glenda's tardiness by asking the boss what time it was just as she walked in the door.*

inalienable (in-AY-lee-un-a-buhl): incapable of being taken away.

> *Although I have always believed freedom of speech to be the INALIENABLE right of every American, I must admit that the diatribes of those who preach hate and violence against members of my race are awfully tough to stomach.*

inanimate (in-AN-ih-mutt): reminiscent of an object that is not alive or animated; lacking in movement.

> *Ben gazed at the wax figure of his dead father as if he expected the INANIMATE figure to come to life.*

inauguration (in-og-yuh-RAY-shun): the act of ushering into office with a formal ceremony; an instance of marking or acknowledging the beginning of something in a ceremonious fashion.

> *President Clinton's INAUGURATION featured a poem composed for the occasion by Maya Angelou and read by the poet.*

inauspicious (in-oss-PISH-uss): accompanied by or predictive of ill luck; not favorable in portent.

> *Who could have predicted that from such INAUSPICIOUS beginnings Grant would rise to command great armies and, eventually, lead his nation?*

incandescent (in-kan-DESS-unt): very bright and hot; brilliant, as light or fire. Also: masterly or dynamic, especially with regard to individual creativity.

> *An INCANDESCENT lamp is one that emits light as a result of the glowing of a heated material, such as a tungsten filament.*

incantation (in-kan-TAY-shun): the repeated chanting of words or phrases believed to have magical powers.

> *I believe Tom's dismissal of the rosary as a primitive set of INCANTATIONS shows how small a role religious faith plays in his life.*

incapacitate (in-kuh-PASS-ih-tate): to disable; to deprive of strength, ability, or skill.

> *Uncle Jimmy missed an entire month of work due to a bout of pneumonia that left him completely INCAPACITATED.*

incendiary (in-SEN-dee-air-ee): flammable. Also, reminiscent of or pertaining to speech or action that is meant to inflame or arouse; deliberately provocative.

> *Adam's INCENDIARY remarks about my mother's parentage resulted in a bloody nose for him and a night in jail for me.*

incipient (in-SIP-ee-unt): early in development; at a beginning stage.

> *Attempting to stave off an INCIPIENT flu, Marsha consumed glass after glass of orange juice.*

incongruous (in-CON-groo-uss): not consistent; incompatible.

> *Much of the troupe's humor relies on an absurd grouping of INCONGRUOUS elements, a technique best exemplified by the dapper-looking, by-the-numbers bureaucrat who heads up the Ministry of Silly Walks.*

incredible (in-KRED-ih-bull): unbelievable; so remarkable as to be hard or impossible to accept. (See, for comparison, the entry for *incredulous*.)

> *The charges I am making against Mr. White may seem INCREDIBLE, but the evidence will show that they are absolutely true.*

incredulous (in-KRED-you-luss): skeptical; refusing or reluctant to believe. (See, for comparison, the entry for *incredible*.)

> *Dan was absolutely INCREDULOUS when I told him I was the sole winner of the $10 million lottery.*

increment (IN-kruh-munt): one in a series of additions; an increase in size or number.

> *The letter informed Nina that she would receive checks from the estate in $50,000 INCREMENTS over the course of twenty years.*

Indiana (in-dee-ANN-uh): the nineteenth state of the United States.

> *The capital of INDIANA is Indianapolis.*

indigent (IN-dih-junt): lacking the essentials of life; impoverished.

> *At the shelter, I came across many INDIGENT families who had fallen victim to the failing economy.*

indignant (in-DIG-nunt): marked by indignation; offended by behavior perceived as unjust or immoral; angered.

> *Although I apologized for the better part of a week for showing up raving drunk at Simon's parent's house, he remained INDIGNANT.*

indict (in-DITE): to charge formally with a crime or offense. (See, for comparison, the entry for *indite*.)

> *Rumors that Mr. Brown would soon be INDICTED for his part in the scandal swept the city.*

indite (in-DITE): to cause to come into being by means of artistic effort; to write or compose. (See, for comparison, the entry for *indict*.)

> *The dozens of letters that passed between the two contained a number of rather steamy poems INDITED under the influence of mutual passion.*

indoctrinate (in-DOCK-truh-nate): to teach; to impart with the knowledge or views of a particular group, philosophy, or theory.

> *Max's earnest attempts to INDOCTRINATE me with the ideals of the Communist Party left me howling with laughter.*

induct (in-DUCT): to install as a member with formal ceremony; to install in office.

> *Many baseball fans feel it's a shame that Pete Rose will probably never be INDUCTED into the Baseball Hall of Fame.*

inert (in-URT): inactive; unmoving; extremely slow in moving or reacting.

> *We came home from the supermarket to find Dad lying INERT on the sofa and the lawn still not mowed.*

influenza (in-floo-EN-zuh): a contagious respiratory virus characterized by inflammation of the mucous membrane, fever, prostration, aches, and pains.

> *David was still weak from his bout with INFLUENZA.*

infuse (in-FYUZE): to fill; to penetrate as if by pouring or soaking.

> *The dynamic commissioner INFUSED a new sense of pride into the beleaguered department.*

ingénue (ON-zhuh-noo): an unworldly, innocent, uncultured young girl; also, an actress who plays such a person.

At age thirty-four, Margo finally had to face the fact that her days of playing INGÉNUES were over.

ingot (ING-gut): a piece of cast metal, usually in the form of a bar.

Charlie's job at the refinery was to inspect the INGOTS coming off conveyor belt number seven.

innuendo (in-you-ENN-doe): a subtle intimation; an indirect insinuation.

Through hints and INNUENDO her opponent managed to plant seeds of doubt about Governor Williams's past.

innumerable (in-NOOM-ur-uh-bul): too many to be numbered or counted (but often used simply to express the idea "very numerous").

Over the past three months, Michelle has put in INNUMERABLE hours of overtime on this project.

inordinate (in-OR-den-it): excessive; too much.

An INORDINATE number of students failed the last test, leading Professor Harris to believe he'd made it too difficult.

insidious (in-SID-ee-uss): designed to entrap; happening or spreading harmfully but subtly; stealthily and seductively treacherous.

Mark's chess games were full of INSIDIOUS traps meant to lull his opponent into a sense of complacency.

135

insinuate (in-SIN-you-ate): to hint at darkly; to suggest (typically, with negative connotations).

> *I hope you don't mean to INSINUATE that my husband is seeing another woman.*

insouciant (in-SOO-see-unt): calm and carefree; indifferent.

> *Despite his dire surroundings, Herbert managed to remain INSOUCIANT and at ease.*

insuperable (in-SOO-pur-uh-bul): impossible to overcome.

> *Faced with hostile rhetoric from members of his own party, mounting opposition in Congress, and a seemingly INSUPERABLE resistance to his policies on the part of the press, the president must sometimes have wondered why he ever selected this line of work.*

insurrection (in-sur-REK-shun): a rebellion against a government or ruling power.

> *Before the president could get the treaty through Congress, however, he would have to attend to an INSURRECTION of sorts that had arisen in the left flank of his own party.*

intangible (in-TAN-juh-bul): incapable of being touched, felt, or calculated.

> *Friends berated me for breaking up with Matthew, but there was something INTANGIBLE missing from the relationship, something I couldn't do without.*

intercede (in-tur-SEED): to offer aid or action on another's behalf; to interrupt (a conflict or altercation) to help another.

> *Much to my amazement, my big brother, whose main goal in life had always seemed to be to torment me, INTERCEDED when the school bully tried to attack me.*

interlope (IN-tur-lope): to intrude; to interfere, meddle, or infringe.

> *Eric resented his fraternity brothers' attempts to INTERLOPE on his romantic evening with Sheena.*

intersperse (in-tur-SPURSE): to scatter here and there; to distribute or place at intervals.

> *INTERSPERSED throughout the studio audience were "clappers" whose sole purpose was to motivate the rest of the crowd into laughing and applauding for the show.*

interstellar (in-tur-STEL-lur): occurring or situated between the stars.

> *Due to problems with the base's satellite transmitter, INTERSTELLAR communication with the space shuttle was extremely difficult.*

interstice (in-TUR-stis): a space between objects; a crevice or crack.

> *Greg shimmied up the INTERSTICE between the two rocks.*

intractable (in-TRACK-tuh-bull): unwilling to be led; stubborn.

> *Although Monty tried everything he could think of to help Elston overcome his habit of exploding at his coworkers, and proved quite INTRACTABLE and actually seemed to resent his efforts.*

intrigue (in-TREEG): to arouse suspicion or curiosity; to engender a sense of mystery. As a noun: a plot.

> *Keith's plan INTRIGUED us, but we had a nagging suspicion it wouldn't work.*

inured (in-YOORD): accustomed to (hardship or trial).

> *After a few months, Melvin became INURED to the paper*
> *boy's habit of tossing the New York* Times *into the*
> *furthest reaches of the front lawn's tall hedges.*

inveigle (in-VAY-gul): to tempt or persuade by using
deception, artful talk, or flattery.

> *My daughter Sharon tried to INVEIGLE me into playing*
> *gin rummy by promising to clean up the kitchen for the*
> *next week, even though she know she'd be at summer camp.*

invert (in-VURT): to reverse; to change to an opposite
orientation or course.

> *After complaining of poor vision all morning, Kathy found*
> *out that her problem was an INVERTED left contact lens.*

invidious (in-VID-ee-uss): likely to damage a reputation.

> *Brent's INVIDIOUS remarks to the president at the*
> *company picnic are probably the main reason he was*
> *passed over for promotion.*

iota (eye-O-tuh): a minute quantity; an extremely small
amount.

> *The fact that the prisoner's reprieve omits his middle*
> *initial doesn't matter one IOTA, Warden Holloway.*

Iowa (EYE-oh-uh): the twenty-ninth state of the United States.

> *The capital of IOWA is Des Moines.*

isthmus (ISS-mus): a narrow strip of land connecting two
larger masses of land.

> *The geologic evidence suggests that, long ago, an*
> *ISTHMUS linked Siberia and Alaska.*

itinerary (eye-TIN-uh-rare-ee): a list of things to be done and seen while on a trip; a summary of the arrivals, departures, and other particulars of one's projected travels.

I had hoped this vacation would give me a chance to relax, but after glancing at the ITINERARY, I feel I'm likely to come back more exhausted than before I left.

its (its): belonging to it. (For comparison, see the entry for *it's*.)

This job of mine has ITS ups and downs.

it's (its): it is. (For comparison, see the entry for *its*.)

IT'S certainly a lovely morning!

jackanapes (JAK-uh-napes): an arrogant or impertinent person; especially, an impudent young man.

If that JACKANAPES tells you to put his photo on the book jacket one more time, it will be the last day he works here as an editor.

jaded (JAY-dud): worn out; dulled or satiated due to overindulgence.

Her parents thought that providing Tracy with everything her heart desired as a child would make her a happy person, but she grew up to be a JADED and selfish woman.

jambalaya (jam-buh-LIE-uh): a spicy Cajun dish featuring rice cooked with ham, sausage, chicken, shrimp, or oysters, and seasoned with herbs.

Anna had so much ham left over from Easter dinner that she decided to try to whip up a JAMBALAYA.

jargon (JAR-gun): the specialized language or vocabulary of a particular profession, trade, or hobby.

Throughout, the book asks the reader to make sense of some rather sophisticated JARGON likely to be comprehensible only to those familiar with accounting procedures.

jaundice (JON-diss): a yellowish tint to the body's skin, fluids, and tissues as a result of the build-up of excessive bile; also, a biased, hostile attitude.

The cosmetics saleswoman tried to convince her that the makeover had given her a tanned, glowing appearance, but Shawna worried that she just looked JAUNDICED.

je ne sais quoi (zheuh-neuh-say-KWAH): from the French for "I don't know what"; a special, intangible quality.

"This ascot you lent me lends a certain . . . JE NE SAIS QUOI," said Edgar, turning to catch himself at a better angle in the mirror."

jeopardize (JEP-ur-dize): to put in danger of being harmed or adversely affected.

Only after he had narrowly avoided being arrested for drunk driving did Marcus realize that his behavior could JEOPARDIZE his future as a lawyer.

jetsam (JET-sum): material thrown overboard to lighten the load of a ship in danger.

As the ship filled with seawater, Madame Fontaine pleaded with the sailor not to throw her trunk of clothes overboard with the rest of the JETSAM sinking beneath the wild waves.

jihad (jee-HAD): an Islamic holy war; a bitter war or dispute entered over a matter of principle.

> *The terminology can be troublesome, Mr. Ambassador; to us it was a terrorist act, but to those sympathetic with the group that planted the bomb it was a holy act undertaken as part of a JIHAD.*

jilt (jilt): to cast (a lover) aside, to discard or dismiss unfeelingly.

> *After being JILTED so abruptly by Michael, Jane found it hard to trust men enough to enter another relationship.*

jingoism (JING-go-iz-um): staunch, extreme patriotism or chauvinism; calculatedly overblown patriotic rhetoric used for political advantage.

> *This kind of JINGOISM has no place in national political discourse, sir!*

jitney (JIT-nee): a small car or bus charging a low fare.

> *Grandpa told us stories of how he used to make his living driving a JITNEY around town.*

jovial (JOE-vee-ul): possessing a joyous, happy nature; good-hearted.

> *Holly's JOVIAL spirit in the face of such adversity was an inspiration to us all.*

jubilation (joo-bih-LAY-shun): extreme joy; a mood of high celebration.

> *Fifteen years in the maternity ward had not dulled the feeling of JUBILATION Doctor Meade experienced every time she helped bring new life into the world.*

juggernaut (JUG-ur-not): an object or force so powerful that it flattens or destroys anything in its path.

The earthquake did some minor structural damage to the city, but the tornado that followed a week late was a JUGGERNAUT, destroying every home and building it touched.

jujitsu (ju-JIT-soo): a Japanese art of unarmed self-defense, the strategy of which is to use an opponent's strength and weight against him or her.

Cornered by a pair of thugs in the alley, Justine was able to call upon her JUJITSU skills to fight her way to safety.

julienne (joo-lee-EN): in thin strips (of vegetables); also, the soup containing such vegetables.

Lisa knew JULIENNE vegetables would look more elegant on the plates of her dinner guests than those cut in the normal way, but she wasn't up for the hours of preparation it would take to slice up carrots and celery for a party of twenty.

juncture (JUNK-chur): a point in time, especially an important one.

"Thank you for your optimism, " said Senator Byron, "but I feel that celebrating my victory at this JUNCTURE would be premature."

junket (JUNK-it): a recreational trip, outing, or excursion; often, a pleasure trip taken by public officials for the ostensible purpose of gathering facts.

The congressman's eight-week trip to Oahu, supposedly to survey the Hawaiian approach to health care, is only the latest of a long series of JUNKETS that call into question his ability to manage public resources with integrity.

Kansas (KAN-zus): the thirty-fourth state of the United States.

> *The capital of KANSAS is Topeka.*

karma (KAR-muh): in Hinduism and Buddhism, the law or force dictating that current circumstances result from one's past actions, decisions, or lifestyle; consequences of one's past. Also: the general principle of cause and effect underlying the operations of the universe.

> *Greg put his car trouble down to the "bad automotive KARMA" that he felt had accompanied him since he overcharged for the used Volkswagen he sold in 1968.*

Kentucky (ken-TUCK-ee): the fifteenth state of the United States.

> *The capital of KENTUCKY is Frankfort.*

kibbutz (ki-BUHTZ): a communal farm in Israel.

> *For her senior year of college, Linda completed a specialized program by living and working on a KIBBUTZ.*

kilter (KIL-tur): working condition; correct position; order.

> *Although I had used a level and ruler when hanging the painting, I could see that it was off-KILTER when I stepped back a few feet.*

kin (kin): one's relatives.

> *Eric was not used to spending such a long period of time away from his KIN in Ohio.*

kiosk (KEE-osk): A small vending booth.

> *Once out of the subway station, I picked up a copy of the New York Times at a newspaper KIOSK.*

kith (kith): one's friends and acquaintances. (Generally used with "kin.")

> *Linda enjoyed her job in Los Angeles, but she was willing to give it up to return to her KITH and kin back in Massachusetts.*

knell (nell): a sound emanating from a bell; the toll of a bell, particularly a bell rung as part of a funeral ceremony.

> *Though she couldn't bring herself to attend her uncle's funeral, Brenda stood on the hill above the graveyard and listened to the KNELL of the church bells.*

kow-tow (KOW-tow): to show respect, deference, or servility.

> *For the sake of keeping peace in the family, Alice KOW-TOWED to her father, spending her evenings at home instead of joining her friends at the dance club.*

kung fu (kung FOO): an Oriental art of self-defense, the strategy of which is to strike quick, successive blows to an opponent's weak spots using fluid hand and leg moves.

> *The mugging shook Adam up so badly that he began taking KUNG FU lessons the next day, hoping to protect himself in the future.*

labyrinth (LAB-uh-rinth): an intricate or oversized maze; any place or situation in which getting one's bearings seems difficult or impossible.

> *As part of his experiment, Herman timed how long it took the various breeds of mice to make it through a LABYRINTH to a dish bearing a piece of cheese.*

lacerated (LASS-uh-ray-tud): cut, torn, ripped, or mangled.

> *Because I LACERATED my finger with the scissors while I was on the job, I was eligible to file a workers' compensation claim.*

lachrymose (LACK-rih-moce): causing tears or sadness.

> *While most men I know dismiss* An Affair to Remember *as a LACHRYMOSE melodrama, the women in my office consider it one of the best movie romances in history.*

lackadaisical (lack-uh-DAZE-ih-kul): lacking spirit or energy; languid.

> *I was feeling rather LACKADAISICAL last Sunday, so I stayed in bed all day and watched football games instead of mowing the lawn.*

lackluster (LACK-lus-tur): dull; not shiny or brilliant.

> *Wanda's LACKLUSTER performance as Hedda Gabler led one critic to remark that she probably had a long career ahead of her in the theater—as a stage weight.*

laity (LAY-uh-tee): a group of religious worshipers differentiated from the clergy; members of the lay community.

> *Bishop Riley, ever mindful that his predecessor had been criticized for his inaccessibility, made a point of mingling with the LAITY as much as possible.*

lalapalooza (la-luh-puh-LOO-zuh): something outstanding or unusual.

> *The charity carnival concluded with a LALAPALOOZA of a parade, in which the mayor rode a unicycle and juggled grapefruits to the sound of wild applause.*

lamina: (LAM-ih-nuh): a thin coating or sheet.

> *The new window came wrapped in a clear plastic LAMINA to protect it.*

lassitude (LASS-ih-tood): a condition of listlessness, exhaustion, or weakness; a feeling of indifference.

> *Mary's uncharacteristic LASSITUDE at work can, I think, be explained by the fact that her father, who is gravely ill, is now living with her.*

latent (LAY-tunt): existing and having the power to become visible or manifest, but for the time being remaining unseen or unknown.

> *The virus remained LATENT in his system for some time, causing him unknowingly to infect those he came in close contact with.*

latke (LOT-kuh): a Jewish potato pancake, often eaten during Hanukkah.

> *Mrs. Bloom always made her famous LATKES for the children during the holiday season.*

lattice (LAT-us): a pattern of crossed wooden or metal strips; any framework or decoration done in this style.

> *The fence in the garden near the main hall was an attractive LATTICE arrangement, apparently broad and discreet, but in fact unforgivingly porous when it came to the intimate conversations of lovers.*

laudable (LAWD-uh-bul): worthy or deserving of praise.

> *Dryly, Professor Helmut told me that my ambition to write the great American novel was LAUDABLE, but that unfortunately my manuscript was a few drafts away from meeting that goal.*

lay (lay): to set something down in a certain position; to place (an object) upon something. (See, for comparison, the entry for *lie*.)

> *Unlike the verb "to lie," the verb "to LAY" must take a direct object, as in "That script really laid an egg."*

lead (led): a metal. Also, as a verb (pronounced "leed"): to take charge or guide. (See, for comparison, the entry for *led*.)

> *Most service stations have stopped selling gasoline containing LEAD.*

led (led): the past tense of the verb "to lead." (See, for comparison, the entry for *lead*.)

> *To our great relief, Vernon LED us out of the forest without a compass.*

leery (LEER-ee): wary; cautious; suspicious.

> *I was LEERY of meeting my friends at the bar downtown: I'd have to travel there by myself on the subway, and there had been several attacks in stations recently.*

legato (leg-AH-toe): in music, possessing a smooth, even, unbroken sound.

> *The soothing LEGATO of the second movement always draws me into a quiet world of reflection.*

legerdemain (lej-ur-duh-MANE): illusions performed by a magician; sleight-of-hand.

> *With his remarkable ability to make everyday objects seem to disappear, the Amazing Mannini was a true master of LEGERDEMAIN.*

lesser (LESS-ur): smaller; littler. (See, for comparison, the entry for *lessor*.)

> *Sometimes in life we must choose the LESSER of two evils.*

lessor (LESS-or): a person or group granting a lease. (See, for comparison, the entry for *lesser*.)

> *The LESSOR must sign the agreement here, Mr. Watkins.*

levitate (LEV-ih-tayt): to float, hover, or rise in the air, particularly as a result of supernatural or magical powers.

> *The audience watched breathlessly as the magician seemed to make his assistant LEVITATE high above the stage.*

lexicography (lex-ih-KOG-ruh-fee): the compiling, writing, and editing of dictionaries.

> *Though he had never intended to pursue a career in LEXICOGRAPHY, Jeremy spent twenty years with Merriam-Webster, working his way up from researcher to editor.*

libel (LIE-bull): a written, printed, or pictorial statement or assertion that is unjustly negative, defaming, or hurtful to one's character and reputation.

> *Several celebrities have sued the supermarket tabloid for LIBEL, but the parade of lurid and preposterous headlines has continued unabated.*

liberal (LIB-uh-rul): generous in giving; tolerant of different ideas and people; in politics, favoring democratic reform; progressive.

> *According to the tourist guide, Mario's was famous for its LIBERAL portions of lasagna, ravioli, and garlic bread.*

libertine (LIB-ur-teen): one who lives life unconcerned and unrestrained by popular convention or morality; a promiscuous person, especially a man.

> *Presumably because he is divorced, my elderly grandmother refers to my fiance Eric as "that LIBERTINE," but everyone else in my family thinks he's wonderful.*

libretto (li-BRET-oh): the text of a musical work, such as a cantata or opera, often accompanied by a translation.

> *As she is fluent in Italian, Maria rarely needs to refer to the LIBRETTO when attending the opera.*

licentious (lie-SENN-shuss): having little or no moral restraint, especially with regard to sex.

> *After months of watching Gary leave the nightclub with one woman after another, Paul finally decided to tell Maureen of her husband's LICENTIOUS behavior.*

lie (lie): to recline; to rest. Also: to tell an untruth. Also: a falsehood (See, for comparison, the entry for *lay*)

> *"I'm just LYING here doing nothing," Rick LIED, pointing to the tiny microphone and motioning for Trudy to keep quiet.*

lieu (loo): place; stead.

> *This year, in LIEU of individual Christmas presents, the five of us took a family vacation to Hawaii.*

limpid (LIM-pid): very clear; transparent.

> *Looking into a LIMPID stream of swift-flowing water, we saw that it was full of migrating salmon.*

lineage (LIN-ee-uj): ancestry; line of descent.

> *A thoroughbred German shepherd from a championship line, my dog Khan probably had a more prestigious LINEAGE than anyone in our family.*

lionize (LIE-uh-nize): to praise excessively; to idolize.

> *For years young baseball fans LIONIZED Babe Ruth, whose many indiscretions were usually overlooked by the press.*

lip-sync (LIP-sink): to simulate a live singing performance by mouthing along to a record.

> *It is common these days for recording artists to LIP-SYNC for the bulk of a "live" concert.*

liqueur (li-KER): an alcoholic beverage flavored with fruit, nuts, seeds, spices, herbs, or a combination of these ingredients.

> *After diner, the hostess gave us a choice of several exotic LIQUEURS; I chose Frangelico because I love the taste of hazelnuts.*

literal (LIT-uh-rul): meaning exactly what is said or written; not open to interpretation.

> *Mr. Pickney's unyielding, LITERAL-minded interpretations of his supervisor's directives left him very little flexibility in handling unanticipated crises in his department.*

lithe (lithe): graceful; supple.

> *LITHE dancers dressed in brilliant gold sprang across the stage to the sound of drums and cymbals.*

loath (loath): unwilling; reluctant. (See, for comparison, the entry for *loathe*.)

> *George wanted to go to the party, but his wife was LOATH to leave little Amy, who had the flu, with a sitter.*

loathe (loathe): to hate or detest. (See, for comparison, the entry for *loath*.)

> *My wife has always LOATHED the Three Stooges, a cultural lapse on her part that I am perfectly willing to forgive.*

lope (lope): a long, galloping stride. As a verb: to move using such a stride.

> *My horse was LOPING along at an easy pace until a car backfired suddenly, causing him to break into a terrified gallop.*

Louisiana (loo-wee-zee-AN-uh): the eighteenth state of the United States.

> *The capital of LOUISIANA is Baton Rouge.*

lowbrow (LOE-brow): uncultured; unsophisticated.

> *Earl's LOWBROW humor may have been fine for his fellow mechanics down at the garage, but his wife did not consider her bridge companions the proper audience for such remarks.*

lucre (LOO-kur): profits; financial rewards; money.

> *After untold hours creating and developing the software program, Miles received only $2,000 for his efforts—a tiny fraction of the LUCRE that poured into company coffers from sales of the product.*

luminary (LOO-mih-nay-ree): something that emits light; also, a person widely renowned and respected in his or her area of expertise.

Among other LUMINARIES who attended the party was the author of this year's Pulitzer winner for drama.

lummox (LUM-ox): a dim-witted and awkward person; an oaf.

Sherman had a heart of gold, but when it came to social etiquette, he was something of a LUMMOX.

lyrical (LEER-ih-kull): musical; flowing; expressive.

The LYRICAL quality of Ash's poetry often masks a harsh, mournful world view.

Machiavellian (mok-ee-uh-VELL-ee-un): relating to the qualities espoused by Machiavelli in *The Prince*; cunning and deceitful in the pursuit of power, particularly with regard to political matters.

Although Lyndon Johnson was certainly a ruthless politician, he was far from the MACHIAVELLIAN figure suggested by some of his biographers.

magnitude (MAG-nih-tood): greatness of size, impact, or extent.

The MAGNITUDE of the task facing the jury became apparent to them only near the end of the trial.

maharajah (mah-huh-RAH-zhuh): formerly, an Indian ruling prince, especially one of a major state.

The MAHARAJAH and his entourage rode into the village on a procession of elephants.

Maine (mane): the twenty-third state of the United States.

The capital of MAINE is Augusta.

maladroit (mal-uh-DROIT): clumsy; uncoordinated.

Having earned a reputation as the most MALADROIT member of the family, Ernie came in for a lot of teasing when he announced his plans to take up figure skating.

malaise (muh-LAZE): a vague feeling of illness, uneasiness, or sadness.

"Sheer idiocy," commented the professor at the end of my paper, in which I argued that Shakespeare's King Lear suffered only a passing MALAISE, not madness.

malapropism (MAL-a-prop-ism): the ridiculous misuse of similar-sounding words.

Bert's reference to the accounting department's "physical prudence" was only one of the morning's many MALAPROPISMS.

malfeasance (mal-FEE-zunce): an instance of breaking the law or otherwise engaging in wrongdoing, particularly with regard to the acts of a public official.

The D.A.'s much-publicized MALFEASANCE during the Cooper case—concealing evidence and manipulating testimony—ended up ruining his political career.

malicious (muh-LISH-uss): spitefully mean; evil; bad in intent.

Fred said his comments were all intended as constructive criticism, but I detected a MALICIOUS note in some of his suggestions.

malign (muh-LINE): to defame; to besmirch (the reputation of).

> *The much-MALIGNED team owner's decision to trade his star quarterback turned out to be one of the best moves he ever made.*

malleable (MAL-ee-uh-bull): shapeable; capable of being molded, changed, or influenced.

> *Senator Green was of the opinion that public opinion was fairly MALLEABLE, and that any scandal, if handled properly, could be overcome.*

manatee (MAN-uh-tee): a large mammal reminiscent of a seal found in shallow waters off the coast of Florida.

> *Unfortunately, the MANATEE has joined the ever-growing list of animals in danger of extinction.*

mandolin (man-duh-LINN): an eight-stringed fretted instrument similar to a lute..

> *Patrick called the MANDOLIN player over to serenade the table while he asked Jeannie for her hand in marriage.*

mar (mar): to spoil, damage, or tarnish.

> *Alissa's birthday party was MARRED by a loud altercation between two motorists on the street outside our house.*

marrow (MARE-oh): the essential part; literally, a vital material that fills the inside of bone cavities.

> *The doctor assured Ellen that, once an appropriate donor was found, her bone MARROW transplant would take place immediately.*

Maryland (MARE-ih-lund): the seventh state of the United States.

The capital of MARYLAND is Annapolis.

marzipan (MAR-zuh-pan): a popular candy made from almonds, egg whites and sugar, often molded into the shapes of animals.

In Europe it is quite common to decorate a Christmas tree with edible decorations, including gingerbread men, MARZIPAN animals, and miniature fruitcakes.

Massachusetts (mass-uh-CHOO-sutts): the sixth state of the United States.

The capital of MASSACHUSETTS is Boston.

material (muh-TEER-ee-ul): physical substance; essence; something from which things are or can be constituted. (See, for comparison, the entry for *materiel*.)

With the right MATERIALS, Dave, we could build a treehouse out back.

materiel (muh-teer-ee-EL): military equipment and weapons. (See, for comparison, the entry for *material*.)

We have solid evidence that enemy MATERIEL has been making it past the embargo, Mr. President.

matriarchy (MAY-tree-ark-ee): a society that traces descent and inheritance through the female line.

If we lived in a MATRIARCHY, the husband and children would probably take the wife's last name.

matrix (MAY-trix): a place, situation, or object that acts as the point of origin or development for something else; a mold.

> *The art department was the MATRIX of all of the company's great creative works.*

maudlin (MAUD-lin): gushingly or tearfully sentimental.

> *I would have liked to believe Kent when he swore I was his dearest friend in the world, but I had a feeling it was all the MAUDLIN babbling of a man who had had a little too much fun at a party.*

maunder (MAWN-dur): to speak or act in an aimless, incoherent fashion.

> *In spite of—or perhaps because of—his father's tendency to be an overachiever, William MAUNDERED through life without the slightest ambition.*

mean (meen): in mathematics, an intermediate value or average of a series of figures. (See, for comparison, the entry for *median*.)

> *The MEAN of the series (0, 3, 6, 7, 9) is five.*

median (MEE-DEE-UN): in mathematics, a middle number in a series of numbers. (See, for comparison, the entry for *mean*.)

> *The MEDIAN of the series (0, 3, 6, 7, 9) is six.*

medley (MED-lee): a group of varying elements; a mixture; in music, a series of songs or melodies connected as one.

> *Dinner at the club that night was especially tasty: chicken piccata, wild rice, and a MEDLEY of winter vegetables.*

melanin: (MEL-uh-nin): a dark pigment found in skin, eyes, and hair.

> *Albino organisms lack MELANIN, and many have white hair, pale skin, and pale, sensitive eyes.*

memento (muh-MEN-toe): a souvenir.

> *I took home a variety of sea shells as MEMENTOS of my beach vacation.*

memoir (MEM-wahr): a series of written reminiscences about people, places, and events composed by and from the point of view of someone with intimate knowledge of the details.

> *The pretense extended even to the former president's MEMOIRS, in which he repeated his assertion that he had no knowledge of how or why the crucial minutes were erased from the tape.*

menagerie (muh-NAZH-uh-ree): a group of wild animals collected for exhibition; any exotic grouping of people or elements.

> *Wilma thought of her eccentric staff not so much as a group of artists, but as a strange MENAGERIE of very creative people who had to be approached with deference.*

mendicant (MEN-dih-kunt): beggar.

> *There, among the castoffs of society, the lepers, MENDICANTS, and prostitutes of the city, he decided to begin his ministry.*

menorah (muh-NORE-uh): a nine-branched candelabrum used during the Jewish festival of Hanukkah.

> *In our office we display both a Christmas tree and a brass MENORAH during the holiday season.*

mercurial (mur-KYOOR-ee-ul): quickly changing; unpredictable.

> *Helen's MERCURIAL temperament often mystified her subordinates, who might find themselves showered with gifts one moment and subjected to verbal abuse the next.*

meritocracy (mare-ih-TOK-ruh-see): a system in which those perceived as talented or intelligent are granted positions of preeminence.

> *Dara, who felt popularity rather than quality of work was the main factor in getting a promotion in her department, snorted when I alluded to a MERITOCRACY.*

meritorious (mare-uh-TORE-ee-uss): worthy of praise, laudable.

> *Earl's work at the homeless shelter was MERITORIOUS, but it left him little time for his family and friends.*

meretricious (mare-uh-TRISH-uss): attracting attention by vulgar, trashy means; false or insincere.

> *Many critics claim that Madonna's success is more the result of her MERETRICIOUS self-promotion talents than her musical talent.*

mete (meet): to measure out; to distribute in proportion.

> *Roland pressed ahead with the case, confident that right would prevail and that justice would eventually be METED out.*

meteor (MEE-tee-or): glowing matter from space, typically stone or metal, that passes through and lights up the sky; a shooting star.

> *Apparently, the vast majority of reported UFOs turn out to be METEORS.*

Michigan (MISH-ih-gun): the twenty-sixth state of the United States.

The capital of MICHIGAN is Lansing.

microfiche (MEYE-kroh-feesh): microfilm that has been converted to small sheets so that it can be read from a special viewing machine.

Seven straight hours at the MICROFICHE machine perusing old newspaper articles on World War II left Elaine blurry-eyed, but with a firm historical sense of the setting of her new novel.

midriff (MID-riff): on the human body, the middle area of the torso; the diaphragm.

Allison wondered if the outfit she had selected was appropriate for meeting her fiance's parents; the shirt barely covered her MIDRIFF.

mien (meen): demeanor; appearance; overall impression.

A punctual man with an attentive, organized MIEN, Tony seemed the ideal candidate for the job.

migraine (MIE-grane): an excruciating headache, caused by expanding capillaries, that occurs on one (usually the left) side of the head, and causes the sufferer nausea, vomiting, and extreme sensitivity to light.

As a treatment for my MIGRAINES, the doctor gave me a new prescription, suggesting I take two tablets and lie down in a very dark room whenever I felt one coming on.

mildew (MIL-doo): a pungent, fungus-like coating forming on paint, cloth, carpet, etc., as a result of excessive exposure to moisture.

> *I remembered too late that I had left my favorite sweater in the washer; after a week of sitting damp in the machine, it stank of MILDEW.*

milieu (meal-YEUH): one's environment; that which surrounds (a person or organism) and affects growth and development.

> *Esther could adapt her behavior to any MILIEU, whether the hustle and bustle of New York city or the slow, easy pace of a quiet seaside village in Maine.*

mimic: (MIM-ik): to imitate (mannerisms or speech), usually in a playful or mocking way.

> *Jerome, who could MIMIC Mr. Harris's squeaky voice with great precision, never missed an opportunity to display his talents to the class when the instructor left the room.*

mince (mince): to chop into small pieces; figuratively, to use evasive or indirect language. Also: to walk affectedly, taking short steps.

> *"Don't MINCE words with me, Henry, " my boss growled; "if you aren't going to meet the deadline, tell me so."*

Minnesota (min-uh-SOE-tuh): the thirty-second state of the United States.

> *The capital of MINNESOTA is St. Paul.*

minotaur (MIN-uh-tore): in mythology, a creature that is part human, part bull.

Half-human, half-animal creatures such as the MINOTAUR, the centaur, and Medusa were pervasive in ancient Greek mythology.

minuscule (MIN-uss-kyool): extremely small.

Sometimes, trying to decipher the MINUSCULE names, numbers, and signs on a map only makes me feel more lost.

mire (mire): waterlogged ground; swampland. Also: any corrupt or unpleasing environment from which it is difficult to extricate oneself. As a verb: to cause to be stuck in mire.

In the early going, the administration found itself MIRED in issues far from its stated goal of improving the economy.

misanthrope (MISS-un-thrope): one who hates mankind or people; a person who expects only the worst in his dealings with others.

In the course of a single night, Scrooge undergoes a remarkable transformation from MISANTHROPE to enlightened benefactor.

miscellany (MISS-uh-lay-nee): a grouping or collection of various elements.

The volume, which featured a hodgepodge of essays, poems, and interviews relating to the Beats, was an intriguing MISCELLANY of writings from the bohemian world of the fifties.

misconstrue (mis-kun-STROO): to get the wrong idea; to misunderstand or misinterpret.

Tom MISCONSTRUED Linda's friendliness as flirting—until he met her boyfriend.

misnomer (miss-NO-mur): an incorrect or inappropriate name.

Vlad the Impaler, the historical antecedent for the Dracula character, was a man apparently intent on demonstrating to the world that his name was no MISNOMER.

Mississippi (miss-uh-SIP-ee): the twentieth state of the United States.

The capital of MISSISSIPPI is Jackson.

Missouri (mih-ZOOR-ee): the twenty-fourth state of the United States.

The capital of MISSOURI is Jefferson City.

modus operandi (MO-duss op-uh-RAN-deye): the mode of operation or style of doing something; from the Latin for "method of operating."

When Jason confessed, the police thought they had their killer, but after careful questioning it became apparent he didn't know anything about the strange MODUS OPERANDI linking the murders, or about the silver cuff link always dropped at the scene of the crime.

modus vivendi (MO-duss vih-VEN-dee): lifestyle; a way of living.

While most envied his rich and seemingly carefree existence, Glen often found his extravagant MODUS VIVENDI rather empty and lonely.

mohair (MO-hair): the hair of the angora goat; fabric or clothing made from this hair.

Rudy loved the MOHAIR sweater I knitted for his birthday, but it gave him a rash.

mon ami (mone-ah-MEE): my friend.

Deadlines come and deadlines go, MON AMI, but you and I remain.

monarchy (MON-ark-ee): government by a single ruler claiming a hereditary right to sovereignty; an example or instance of perceived royal lineage.

King George III's troubled reign, highlighting the disadvantages of MONARCHY as a form of government, was characterized by civil unrest in the colonies, mental incapacity in the sovereign, and the usual pack of useless hangers-on at court.

moniker (MON-ih-kur): name; nickname.

The rock star Sting has revealed in interviews that even his parents and children refer to him by his famous MONIKER.

mononucleosis (mon-oh-noo-klee-OH-siss): an infectious illness caused by an increase of mononuclear levkocytes in the blood, and characterized by extremely swollen glands, a sore throat, and exhaustion.

Erika's MONONUCLEOSIS caused her to miss nearly two months of school.

monophonic (mon-uh-FON-ik): of or pertaining to sound reproduction using a single signal channel.

Although the group's recordings were released for MONOPHONIC systems, the new compact disc features stereo remixes of their most famous songs.

monosyllabic (mah-no-sih-LAB-ik): having only one syllable.

We tried to engage Kathleen in conversation but couldn't get more than MONOSYLLABIC grunts for our pains.

163

monotonous (muh-NOT-uh-nuss): failing to excite interest; boring, tedious, repetitive and dull; literally, possessing only one tone or note.

Mike admitted that screwing the caps on soda bottles on an assembly line was MONOTONOUS work, but he claimed it paid surprisingly well.

Montana (mon-TAN-uh): the forty-first state of the United States.

The capital of MONTANA is Helena.

morass (muh-RASS): a quagmire; a difficult or bewildering situation.

By 1973 the military was more eager than ever before to extricate itself from the MORASS in Southeast Asia.

mordant (MOR-duhnt): bitingly sarcastic; cynical.

Thelma had a MORDANT wit that could stop the most arrogant swaggerer in his tracks.

mountebank (MOUNT-uh-bank): a charlatan; one who sells worthless medicines, potions, and the like; a fake.

The line between visionary romantic and common MOUNTEBANK, for my father, was often a thin one.

munitions (myoo-NISH-unz): the materials of war; weapons or ammunition.

Neil felt his training with the army's MUNITIONS unit put him in good standing for a position with the police department's bomb squad.

nadir (NAY-dur): the lowest point.

The NADIR of my writing career was probably that spell in Omaha when I wrote obituaries for the local newspaper.

nanosecond (NAN-o-sek-und): One billionth of a second; an extremely short period of time.

It seemed the phone was on the hook for only a NANOSECOND before it rang again.

natatorium (nay-tuh-TOR-ee-um): an indoor swimming pool.

Although he had swum in hundreds of venues, Melvin still had a dream of competing in the world's largest NATATORIUM.

nautical (NAW-tih-kul): of the sea, ships, or sailors.

Mr. Petry's den is decorated in a NAUTICAL motif, featuring wallpaper with anchors, paintings of colonial ships, and an authentic ship's wheel hanging on the wall.

Nebraska (nuh-BRASS-kuh): the thirty-seventh state of the United States.

The capital of NEBRASKA is Lincoln.

nebulous (NEB-yuh-luss): cloudy; vague.

Every time Claudia tried to ask Philip about his intentions or the future of their relationship, he gave a NEBULOUS reply and changed the subject.

nefarious (nih-FARE-ee-uss); openly evil; wicked.

The NEFARIOUS Darth Vader serves as the unforgettable villain of George Lucas's Star Wars.

negate (nih-GATE): to cause to be ineffectual; to deny.

I imagine that double hot fudge sundae I ate completely NEGATED the effects of my morning exercises.

nelson (NEL-sun): in wrestling, a kind of hold in which one places one's arm under the opponent's arm and applies pressure to the back of the opponent's neck.

> *When I got Frank in a full NELSON, I knew I would win the match.*

neologism (nee-OL-uh-jiz-um): a newly coined term or word.

> *The computer revolution has spawned not only new technologies but a wealth of NEOLOGISMS, such as "download" and "system crash," that have quickly become part of our workday vocabulary.*

nepotism (NEP-uh-tiz-um): the practice of favoring relatives.

> *The company practiced shameless NEPOTISM, regularly passing up qualified applicants and hiring the underqualified sons, daughters, and cousins of board members.*

n' est-ce pas (ness PAH): from the French "Is it not so?"; "Correct?"

> *"Well, class," our French teacher said, "since you all spent the weekend studying, this test should be a breeze, N'EST-CE PAS?"*

Nevada (nuh-VA-duh): the thirty-sixth state of the United States.

> *The capital of NEVADA is Carson City.*

New Hampshire (noo HAMP-shur): the ninth state of the United States.

> *The capital of NEW HAMPSHIRE is Concord.*

New Jersey (noo JUR-zee): the third state of the United States.

The capital of NEW JERSEY is Trenton.

New Mexico (noo MEX-ih-koe): the forty-seventh state of the United States.

The capital of NEW MEXICO is Santa Fe.

New York (noo YORK): the eleventh state of the United States.

The capital of NEW YORK is Albany.

niggling (NIG-ling): petty; annoying.

I could usually deal with my roommate's NIGGLING complaints about hairs in the sink and my forgetting to take out the trash, but I was in no mood for it today.

nihilism (NIE-uh-liz-im): the belief that life is meaningless.

A profound NIHILISM seems to have fallen over the poet during the last six months she spent in London; her letters to her mother indicate a severe depression.

nimbus (NIM-bus): a halo-like source of light above the head of a saint or spiritual figure.

The mosaic depicts Christ and his disciples with bright NIMBUSES.

noggin (NOG-in): a small drinking vessel; a mug.

Dinner at our favorite seaport restaurant always began with a generous helping of clam chowder served in old-fashioned ceramic NOGGINS.

noisome (NOY-sum): ill-smelling and offensive; also, harmful.

That NOISOME gang of unwashed hooligans you call your friends will bring you to nothing but trouble, Steve.

nolo contendere (NO-lo kun-TEND-er-ee): in law, a plea that admits no guilt, but subjects the defendant to penalty. (Literally, "I am unwilling to contend.")

Charged with income tax evasion, Vice-President Spiro Agnew pleaded NOLO CONTENDERE, to the perfect satisfaction of the Internal Revenue Service.

nomad (NO-mad): one who roams from place to place, having no real roots or home.

Ever since Grandma and Grandpa retired and sold their home, they've lived like NOMADS, traveling the country in a reconditioned Winnebago.

nom de plume (nom duh PLOOM): an author's pseudonym or pen name.

The writer Samuel Langhorne Clemens is better known by his NOM DE PLUME, Mark Twain.

nondescript (non-duh-SKRIPT): not having a particularly distinctive or interesting appearance; hard to describe.

With all the cars on the lot to choose from, Peggy went and picked a NONDESCRIPT grey sedan.

nonillion (no-NILL-yun): a very large number equal to 10,000,000,000,000,000,000,000,000,000,000.

My parents' claim that they had asked me to clean the garage one NONILLION times struck me as the sort of irresponsible exaggeration that relieved me of any obligation to do my chores.

nonpartisan (non-PAR-tih-zun): not a member of a party (political group) or association; unbiased.

> *Although the commission was supposed to be NONPARTISAN, Martin knew for a fact that three of the members were dyed-in-the-wool Democrats who would never vote against the interests of their party.*

North Carolina (north kare-uh-LINE-uh): the twelfth state of the United States.

> *The capital of NORTH CAROLINA is Raleigh.*

North Dakota (north duh-KO-tuh): the thirty-ninth state of the United States

> *The capital of NORTH DAKOTA is Bismarck.*

nota bene (NOTE-ah BEN-eh): a term used to draw attention to a particular point; Latin for "note well." (Sometimes rendered as "N.B.")

> *Applications will be accepted until the first of the month, provided, NOTA BENE, that they are accompanied by an income tax return filed within the last two years.*

notoriety (noe-tuh-RIE-uh-tee): fame; wide publicity (particularly for sensational reasons); also, having an unfavorable reputation.

> *The musical gained NOTORIETY as word spread that it featured bawdy songs and plenty of nudity.*

nougat (NOO-gut): a type of candy containing nuts and honey.

> *The new candy bar contained an appealing mixture of NOUGAT, caramel, and milk chocolate.*

novice (NOV-iss): one who is new to a profession, trade, or sport; a beginner.

You shouldn't take too much pride in having checkmated me in twelve moves, Steve; I'm a NOVICE and you're a nationally rated player.

nullify (NULL-ih-fie): to make invalid; to render null.

Because the league NULLIFIED the disputed home run, the two teams had to play the ninth inning over again the following week.

obsolete (ob-suh-LEET): no longer useful or in use; unnecessary.

The room-sized computers of the sixties have long since been rendered OBSOLETE by the advent of desktop and even laptop equivalents.

obstreperous (ob-STREP-er-us): uncontrollably aggressive; defiant, boisterous.

Before announcing the plan for massive layoffs to his workers, the boss hired an extra security force to prevent certain OBSTREPEROUS persons from inciting a riot.

obtain (ub-TANE): to get or acquire.

With his green card set to expire in a few months, Olaf searched for an American woman who could marry him so that he could OBTAIN citizenship.

ocher (OAK-ur): a yellow or reddish-brown clay; the color typical of this clay.

The shelves of the pottery shop were filled with dozens of OCHER vessels of varying sizes.

ochlophobia (ok-luh-FO-be-uh): an illogical fear or dread of crowds.

Betty never realized she suffered from OCHLOPHOBIA until she moved to the city, where she had great difficulty walking to and from work during rush hour.

octave (OK-tuv): in Western music, a tone eight tones above or below another tone.

The famous opera singer had a vocal range of three OCTAVES.

oenophile (EE-nuh-file): a wine connoisseur.

Len, a lifelong OENOPHILE, shuddered as I produced a bottle of Ripple to accompany our dinner of fish sticks and macaroni and cheese.

off-color (off-KUH-lur): questionable in taste or propriety; distasteful.

The comedienne was talented, but her frequent use of OFF-COLOR remarks kept her from getting bookings on network television shows.

off-the-record (off-the-REK-erd): Not intended for publication.

Senator Power's frank admission that he had never read the United States Constitution was probably intended as an OFF-THE-RECORD comment.

ogle (OH-gul): to watch intently; to gaze at lasciviously.

Bryan's idea of an afternoon well spent was lounging around the beach OGLING women twenty years too young for him.

ogre (O-gur): a legendary man-eating monster; a brute or wicked person.

> *As a child, Vern believed that a huge OGRE lived in his bedroom closet.*

Ohio (oh-HI-oh): the seventeenth state of the United States.

> *The capital of OHIO is Columbus.*

Oklahoma (oke-luh-HOME-uh): the forty-sixth state of the United States.

> *The capital of OKLAHOMA is Oklahoma City.*

olfactory (ol-FAK-tuh-ree): relating to the sense of smell.

> *For me, walking past the bakery every morning on the way to school was an OLFACTORY delight.*

oligarchy (OLL-ih-gark-ee): government by an elite few.

> *My father's opinion was that since the mid-Sixties the country had been operating under the pretense of democracy, and was in fact an OLIGARCHY.*

omnibus (OHM-nih-bus): something that covers many areas or subjects; also, a bus.

> *The OMNIBUS law passed shortly after the publication of Sinclair's The Jungle was meant to assure consumers that blatant violations of basic health and quality standards would never again be seen in the food industry.*

omnidirectional (om-nee-duh-REK-shun-ul): capable of receiving or transmitting from every direction.

> *Agent Warren hid a tiny OMNIDIRECTIONAL microphone in the suspected drug smuggler's hotel room.*

oncology (on-KOL-uh-jee): the study of tumors.

> *Abbey was worried when she found a lump in her breast, but the ONCOLOGY specialist told her it was a benign cyst.*

ontogeny (on-TAHJ-uh-nee): the cycle of development of an organism.

> *The chapter Anne was having trouble with described the ONTOGENY of the common housefly in minute detail, with particular emphasis on the maggot stage.*

ontology (on-TOLL-uh-jee): the study of existence or being.

> *Phoebe was pretty sure of her decision to major in philosophy, but she couldn't decide whether to concentrate in existentialism or ONTOLOGY.*

opacity (oh-PASS-ih-tee): degree of imperviousness to light; level of opaqueness.

> *The paper was of a very low OPACITY, nearly transparent.*

operatic (op-uh-RAT-ik): relating to or reminiscent of the opera; overly dramatic or difficult to believe.

> *I'm afraid my family's conflict style tends to be a little OPERATIC at times.*

opiate (OPE-ee-ut): an addictive narcotic, especially one with numbing or sleep-inducing qualities.

> *Marx's well-known remark that religion is the OPIATE of the people helped make many church groups implacable enemies of Communism.*

oracular (or-AK-yuh-lur): resembling an oracle; said in a solemn or cryptic manner.

> *My boss, Mr. Twombey, always issued his pronouncements in a gloomy, ORACULAR fashion that left us wondering whether something horrible was about to happen.*

orator (ORE-uh-tur):a gifted and persuasive professional public speaker.

> *Don's encyclopedic knowledge of the topic, combined with his ability as an ORATOR, made him the odds-on favorite to win the debate.*

oratorio (or-uh-TOR-ee-oh): a musical piece for voices and instruments that tells a story without the use of costumes or props.

> *Julian preferred ORATORIOS to operas, claiming that the melodramatic plot twists and elaborate costumes of the latter made it hard for him to enjoy the music.*

ordnance (ORD-nunce): weapons; military supplies.

> *Though the government denied there would be a confrontation with the rebels, the reports of dramatically increased ORDNANCE shipments led the press to believe otherwise.*

Oregon (OR-ih-gun): the thirty-third state of the United States.

> *The capital of OREGON is Salem.*

orgiastic (ore-jee-ASS-tick): reminiscent of or pertaining to an orgy; likely to elicit extremely intense emotions.

> *When the doors opened the shoppers streamed into the store in an ORGIASTIC frenzy, hurrying to find the sale's best bargains.*

orifice (ORE-ih-fiss): an opening in the body.

> *The ORIFICE Prince Hamlet makes the Player King select as the receptacle for poison, his victim's ear, recalls the method Claudius used in killing Hamlet's father.*

origami (or-ih-GAH-mee): the Japanese art of cutting and folding paper.

> *After studying ORIGAMI in her craft class, Aunt Janice decided to decorate her entire Christmas tree with miniature paper figures.*

ornery (ORE-nuh-ree): stubborn or unyielding; inclined toward obstinate behavior.

> *Grandma insists that Grandpa was an easygoing fellow in his youth, but since their move from the country he has become quite ORNERY.*

ornithology (or-nih-THAHL-uh-jee): the study of birds.

> *Her lifelong love of birds led Stella to seek a degree in ORNITHOLOGY.*

orotund (OR-uh-tund): (of the voice or speech,) possessing a full, big sound; sonorous; (of a style of speaking) overbearing or pretentious.

> *The senator delivered an impassioned, if OROTUND, defense of the party's trade policy.*

Orwellian (or-WELL-ee-un): resembling the qualities or subject matter of the writing of George Orwell, particularly the totalitarian future world of his book *1984*.

> *My father saw the surveillance cameras in suburban supermarkets as the first sign of an ORWELLIAN clampdown on civil liberties.*

175

oscillate (OSS-ih-late): to sway back and forth; vacillate.

My two-year-old nephew was mesmerized by the fishtank, with its colorful fish, OSCILLATING plants, and soft lighting.

osmosis (oss-MOE-sis): gradual absorption, assimilation.

Jerry rested his head on the textbook and closed his eyes, as if hoping to absorb the information in it by OSMOSIS.

osteoporosis (oss-tee-oh-puh-ROE-sis): a condition of fragile, brittle bones, particularly common in women of advanced age.

The doctor advised all of his female patients over fifty to make sure they took in plenty of calcium as a precaution against OSTEOPOROSIS.

outré (oo-TRAY): strange, eccentric.

For the uninitiated, Kate's performance art may seem rather OUTRÉ; however, she has a dedicated following of people who consider her work very compelling.

oxymoron (ahk-see-MORE-on): a phrase in which contradictory or incongruous terms are used together, as in the phrase "poor little rich kid."

When Ted said the term "military intelligence" always struck him as an OXYMORON, he meant it as a joke, but his cousin, a lifelong army officer, took grave offense.

pact (pakt): an agreement or promise.

When they were each ten years old, Louise and Barbara made a solemn PACT to grow up together, attend the same college, work for the same company, and live in the same house.

palatial (puh-LAY-shul): having the grand, luxurious characteristics of a palace; resembling a palace.

> *Mr. Laramie offered to hold the reception at his PALATIAL seaside mansion, but the social committee opted for a hotel ballroom in the city.*

palisade: (pal-ih-SADE): a defensive barrier or fence comprising a row of tall stakes driven into the ground; also, a line of steep cliffs along a river.

> *As we drove along the PALISADES of the river gorge, my wife and I lamented that we had forgotten to bring our camera.*

palindrome (PAL-in-drome): a word or sentence (such as *pop* or *Not so, Boston*) that reads the same forward and backward.

> *James's dogged attempt to write a novel consisting solely of a single sixty-thousand-word PALINDROME led his relatives to wonder whether his best days as a writer of fiction were behind him.*

pallid (PAL-id): wan, pale; lacking bright, deep color.

> *Frazier's PALLID complexion and inability to bear even the slightest noise led me to conclude that he was hung over.*

palpitate (PAL-pih-tate): to flutter; to beat more rapidly than usual.

> *Mel's heart PALPITATED wildly at the prospect of a date with Irma.*

paltry (PAHL-tree): trivial; insignificant; worthless.

> *The PALTRY sum found in the cash register made us regret having picked this store for our first robbery.*

panacea (pan-uh-SEE-uh): a cure-all; something with the ability to cure any illness or remedy any disorder.

According to my eighty-four-year-old grandfather, chocolate is the PANACEA to any problem life may throw at you.

panache (puh-NASH): a distinctive flair or style; a flamboyant manner.

Rosamund was swept away by the charming stranger's PANACHE—he seemed so dashing and romantic.

panegyric (pan-uh-JIE-rik): a writing or oration intended to praise someone or something.

At her funeral, Erma's grandson read a PANEGYRIC detailing her accomplishments, her kindness, and her love for life.

panjandrum (pan-JAN-drum): an important person; a bigwig.

I was able to obtain a list of local business PANJANDRUMS to solicit for investment funds.

panorama (pan-uh-RAM-uh): an extensive, unobstructed view of a wide area.

Despite my lifelong aversion to flying, I couldn't help admiring the breathtaking PANORAMA of San Francisco below me.

pantomime (PAN-tuh-mime): the conveyance of ideas, words, emotions, or stories without the use of words.

My attempt to describe the accident in PANTOMIME to the villagers I encountered was pathetic; I bitterly regretted my decision not to study French before our trip.

parable (PARE-uh-bull): a brief allegory or story meant to highlight an essential truth.

Jesus' PARABLE of the Prodigal Son is perhaps the most inspiring passage in the New Testament.

paramount (PARE-uh-mount): supreme; superior; excellent.

It is of PARAMOUNT importance that we complete this project on time.

paramour (PARE-uh-more): an illicit lover.

Although the women in her circle made high-minded speeches about her morality, Mrs. Able knew full well that most of them had had a PARAMOUR at one time or another.

paraphernalia (pare-uh-fur-NALE-ee-uh): one's possessions; accessory items relating to a particular profession, hobby, or activity.

The abundance of drug PARAPHERNALIA found in his hotel room did not do much to support the rock star's claim that he abstained from all intoxicating substances on religious grounds.

paraphrase (PARE-uh-frase): to restate in different words. Also, as a noun: an instance of such restating.

To call this work a new translation of the original Greek texts is an overstatement; it is a capable, but by no means groundbreaking, PARAPHRASE of existing English editions.

pariah (puh-RIE-uh): an outcast; one who is shunned, avoided, or despised.

After his firing, Milton had the nerve to show up unannounced at the company picnic, then seemed surprised when he was treated as a PARIAH.

parody (PARE-uh-dee): a satirically humorous imitation or mocking interpretation of a well known work, person, or institution.

"Life in Hell" is an irreverent PARODY of parents, school, and the working world.

paraffin (PARE-uh-finn): a white wax-like material used in the production of candles and wax paper.

So many customers had ordered Betty's homemade Christmas candles that she had to send her son Wally out to buy more PARAFFIN.

partake (par-TAKE): to participate and share in.

Your offer is kind, but I'm under strict doctor's orders not to PARTAKE of any alcoholic beverage.

partisan (PAR-tih-zun): showing a marked inclination or bias. Also, as a noun: one who is partial to a particular side or view.

As a Democrat, I realize that my PARTISAN role in opposing the Governor's policies may cause some of the Republicans in this body to doubt my truthfulness in this matter.

passé (pass-SAY): no longer fashionable or current.

Marge's insistence that platform shoes were PASSÉ led me to believe that she hadn't been keeping up with fashion trends.

passim (PASS-im): a word used to indicate that a given source or element is used frequently throughout a written work.

References to a fictitious writer named Kilgore Trout appear PASSIM in a number of Kurt Vonnegut's novels.

pâté (pah-TAY): a spread or paste made of liver.

I was reluctant to try Roseanne's PÂTÉ, but Michael said I would hurt her feelings if I didn't at least have a bite.

patriarchy (PAY-tree-ark-ee): a group ruled by a patriarch; an organization or clan in which lines of descent and inheritance are traced through the male.

Martha accused her father of running a PATRIARCHY, arguing that she deserved to take on the leadership of the company far more than her younger brother.

patsy (PAT-see): someone who is set up to take the blame of a crime or wrongdoing; one who is framed.

Although conspiracy theorists have seized on Lee Oswald's description of himself as a PATSY, other observers remain unconvinced that he acted as part of an organized plot to kill President Kennedy.

pedant (PED-unt): a person who displays learning inappropriately or excessively; also, someone who focuses too narrowly on rules and minor details.

Don't get Roland started on Shakespearean tragedy; he's a shameless PEDANT who'll dominate an entire lunch hour's discussion with observations on the time problem in Othello.

peerless (PEER-luss): without peer; above others with regard to ability or quality; beyond compare.

Mrs. Reilly's PEERLESS skills as a mediator soon earned her a special position of respect on the school board.

penal (PEE-nul): related to or pertaining to punishment or imprisonment; having to do with a prison system.

President Clinton once remarked that the White House, in his view, represented the crown jewel of the federal PENAL system.

penchant (PEN-chunt): a liking or inclination.

Over dinner, Vicky, who had a PENCHANT for speaking her mind no matter what, asked the congressman what he thought his chances were of being imprisoned as a result of his recent indictment for embezzlement.

penitent (PEN-ih-tunt): feeling guilty or remorseful for wrongdoing. As a noun: a person who is penitent.

Aaron made a token effort to apologize for his rude behavior, but it was evident to us all that he was not at all PENITENT.

Pennsylvania (penn-sil-VANE-yuh): the second state of the United States.

The capital of PENNSYLVANIA is Harrisburg.

pensive (PEN-siv): thoughtful; having wistful or dreamy thoughts.

My girlfriend was ready for a riotous night on the town, but I was feeling, PENSIVE, so we ended up going to a cafe and talking well into the night.

penury (PEN-you-ree): extreme poverty.

Not many of us would be willing to exchange our lot in life for the simple life of PENURY taken on by these monks.

peony (PEE-uh-nee): a colorful plant bearing large petals; the state flower of Indiana.

The florist assembled a lovely arrangement of PEONIES for Aunt Irene.

percolate (PUR-kuh-layt): to pass or make pass through a porous body.

I was dying for a cup of fresh brewed coffee, but as I didn't have time to wait for it to PERCOLATE, I had to settle for instant.

perforated (PUR-fur-aye-tud); featuring holes or opening, especially at regular intervals.

The magazine coupon was PERFORATED along the side for easy removal.

pernicious (pur-NISH-uss): harmful or destructive in nature.

Although the pesticide in question does safely prevent wheat from being ravaged by insects when used alone, environmentalists argue that it is PERNICIOUS—even lethal—when combined with other common farm compounds.

perpetrate (PURP-uh-trate); to be guilty of or responsible for (a misdeed).

I promise you, Mr. Mayor, that we will find the vandals who have PERPETRATED these crimes against the city and make them pay.

perquisite (PURK-wuh-zit): an incidental privilege other than payment that accompanies a position of responsibility; also, an extra payment beyond what is owed. Often shortened to "perk."

Among the president's PERQUISITES were two front-row seats to all the Celtics' regular-season home games.

perjury (PUR-juh-ree): to lie purposely while under oath.

Rather than risk PERJURY charges by lying to the Senate committee, the witness was advised to refuse to answer questions pertaining to his activities in Central America.

pestle (PESS-ul): a tool used to grind substances into a powder in a mortar.

During the excavation, the crew discovered a number of ancient food preparation items, including wooden PESTLES, clay crocks, and eating utensils made of polished bone.

petit four (PET-ee FORE): a small decorated cake. Plural: petits fours.

Aunt Marcia always served tea and PETITS FOURS at three o'clock.

petrified (PET-ruh-fied): scared to the point of losing the ability to move; scared stiff; turned to stone.

My aunt was so PETRIFIED of snakes that when one slithered its way onto the pool deck, my brothers and I had to carry her, lounge chair and all, into the house.

pettifoggery (pet-ee-FOG-er-ee): petty dishonesty or trickery.

"Let's put all this PETTIFOGGERY behind us," said Mr. Powers, "and start dealing with each other in a more straightforward manner."

phaeton (FAY-ih-tin): a lightweight four-wheeled passenger carriage drawn by horses.

The PHAETON, once a common sight on any city street, was eventually phased out and replaced by the automobile.

phallic (FAL-ik): of or pertaining to the phallus or penis; reminiscent of a penis; also, by extension, reminiscent of the life-giving force of nature, as in ancient Dionysian festivals that made the phallus a central element.

According to Freud, PHALLIC symbols (such as the sword of Unferth used by Beowulf) abound in both ancient and modern literature.

phantasmagoria (fan-taz-muh-GORE-ee-uh): a dreamlike, constantly changing series of visions.

The avant-garde film had no dialogue or plot in the traditional sense; it was essentially a PHANTASMAGORIA set to music.

pheromone (FARE-uh-mone): a substance released by an animal that produces specific physiological reactions or behavioral changes in other animals of the same species.

The perfume company's claim that its new perfume contained PHEROMONES that would cause it to act as a human aphrodisiac was the subject of strict scrutiny by federal regulators.

phlegmatic (fleg-MAT-ic): having a calm, unexcitable temperament.

Allan's PHLEGMATIC personality was certainly helpful during the deadline crunch in keeping us all from panicking.

philter (FIL-tur): a magical love potion.

Thinking the glass contained Evian water, Veronica drained the PHILTER to its dregs; her eyes met those of the startled butler, and she melted with tenderness.

phonics (FON-iks): the study of the sounds and acoustics of language.

David's teacher's insistence that studying PHONICS was not necessary to develop good reading skills struck us as odd.

phraseology (fray-zee-ah-LO-jee): in language, the way phrases and words are employed.

With her excellent diction, articulation, and PHRASEOLOGY, Holly had a gift for public speaking and debate.

pictorial (pick-TOR-ee-ul): relating to or consisting of pictures.

National Geographic offers a PICTORIAL introduction to people and cultures we may never have known about before.

pigment (PIG-munt): a dry coloring substance meant to be mixed with fluid; any matter that produces color.

The use of PIGMENTS developed only in the late nineteenth century is proof positive that this painting is not one of Vermeer's.

pilaf (PEEL-af): a flavored rice dish served alone or with meat, poultry, or vegetables.

The restaurant is certainly trying to cater to the needs of the health-conscious, offering more chicken, fish and vegetable entrées than before, and allowing diners a choice of rice PILAF or fries.

pilfer (PIL-fer): to take without authorization or permission; to steal.

I had a feeling the tickets Wayne was trying to sell me had been PILFERED from someone, but he assured me that was not the case.

186

pious (PIE-uss): devout; dedicated to God and the practice of one's faith or religion.

> *Joseph had always seemed to be the most PIOUS of all of us, so no one in our class was surprised when he announced that he'd found his calling in the ministry.*

piquant (pi-KONT): stimulating; provocative, particularly to the tastebuds; spicy.

> *Normally, Mexican food is too hot for me, but Nancy's salsa dip was just PIQUANT enough to be delightful.*

pithy (PITH-ee): something very brief but meaningful and concise.

> *The guest speaker limited his remarks to a few PITHY observations on the impossibility of getting anything done in Washington.*

pittance (PIT-unce): a very small amount.

> *My allowance in those days, of course, was a PITTANCE compared to my brother's.*

pixie (PIK-see): an elf or fairy.

> *The villages believed the mysterious theft to be the work of mischievous PIXIES and trolls.*

placard (PLACK-urd): a notice or sign set out on stiff paper or board.

> *The umpire asked us to remove our PLACARD from the bleacher wall, claiming that it obstructed the view of the hitters.*

plaintive (PLAIN-tive): expressing sorrow or sadness; mournful.

A PLAINTIVE feeling hung over the house for weeks after our dog Sasha died.

plaited (PLAY-tud): braided.

Julia usually wore her hair neatly PLAITED, but she drew more than a few looks when she let it fall to its full length—nearly to her waist—for the company party.

playa (PLY-uh): the lowest area of a desert, usually flat and sometimes covered with water.

The desert's undrained PLAYA contained the only water for hundreds of miles.

plebeian (pluh-BEE-un): everyday, common; reminiscent of or pertaining to persons not part of an elite.

Rather than describing her tastes as PLEBEIAN, Joe, I would have broken off the affair by saying that yours was a love that was meant to flash for a moment, not burn forever.

plebiscite (PLEB-uh-site): a direct public vote on an issue of importance.

Although nonbinding, the PLEBISCITE on the question of statehood was the most bitterly fought campaign in the island's history.

pliable (PLIE-uh-bull): able to be changed in shape, form, or inclination; capable of being directed or influenced.

Gold, one of the world's most valuable metals, is also one of the most PLIABLE.

plod (plod): to trudge along slowly, as if weighed down.

The tour guide noticed Nelson PLODDING along behind the rest of the group and guessed that he was not a big fan of Monet.

plucky (PLUK-ee): brave; courageous.

It was the gnomelike Mario, the last person Sergeant Denton would have termed a PLUCKY young cadet, who ended up winning a medal for risking his own life to save his comrades.

pneumatic (noo-MAT-ik): related to air or wind; using air or compressed gas as a force.

It took Milton some time to master the controls of the huge PNEUMATIC drill, but eventually he got the hang of it and set about a gleeful, early-morning destruction of the pavement outside his absent neighbor's home.

poise (poyze): stability of outlook or emotional state, especially when facing trying circumstances. Also, as a verb: to set on a potentially hazardous surface, such as a narrow edge.

Ruth-Anne's POISE during the rigorous interview impressed us all.

politick (POL-ih-tik): to talk about or engage in politics.

Barry spends hours POLITICKING with his associates.

polydipsia (pol-ee-DIP-see-uh): an abnormal or excessive thirst.

The bartender, clearly uninterested in Ralph's claim to suffer from POLYDIPSIA, told him flatly that he'd had enough.

polygamy (puh-LIG-uh-mee): the societal practice of having more than one spouse (especially, more than one wife) at a time.

> *The sect's advocacy of POLYGAMY and group parenting eventually brought it into bitter conflict with the stern-minded townsfolk of Harris Hollow.*

polygraph (POL-ee-graff): a machine used in lie detection that indicates changes in pulse, perspiration, blood pressure, and respiration.

> *After the suspect passed a series of POLYGRAPH test, police formally dropped all charges.*

pompadour (POMP-uh-dore): a male hairstyle in which the hair is set high in a wave in the front.

> *Don wore a POMPADOUR, a black leather jacket, and blue jeans to the costume party in imitation of his hero Fonzie from "Happy Days."*

pompous (POM-puss): pretentious; overblown; self-important.

> *The food was good and the service was prompt, but our waiter's POMPOUS air and unceasing sneer made me consider leaving a single penny as a tip.*

pongee (pon-JEE): a thin, unbleached variety of silk.

> *The gauze-like scarf was woven from a delicate PONGEE.*

pontiff (PON-tiff): a high or chief priest; usually, the pope.

> *Although lately John Paul II has not made as many pilgrimages to foreign lands as he did in the late Seventies and early Eighties, the PONTIFF has made a special point of visiting one or two important cities per year.*

porcine (PORE-sein): reminiscent of or pertaining to a pig; resembling a pig.

> *Mike's constant description of his heavyset blind date as "my PORCINE companion" may have had something to do with her early departure from the party.*

postern (POSS-turn): a back or rear door or gate, especially in a castle or fort.

> *The fire marshall was unimpressed with our evacuation plan, which required guests, in the event of an emergency, to make their way through a dark, narrow hallway leading to a POSTERN.*

postpartum (post-PAR-tum): occurring after pregnancy and birth.

> *In the weeks following the delivery, Janice felt quite low at times, but her obstetrician assured her that hers was a standard case of POSTPARTUM depression and would soon pass.*

potent (PO-tunt): strong; powerful.

> *The poor review of Henry's play served as a POTENT incentive for him to labor more carefully over the next one.*

prattle (PRAT-ul): meaningless babble; idle chatter.

> *I had stopped at the diner to have breakfast and read the morning paper, but the endless PRATTLE of the waitress made it impossible for me to get beyond the front page.*

precedence (PRESS-uh-dunce): the act or right of preceding; an instance or claim of coming first in order or priority.

> *To his credit, the president of the toy company agreed that the safety of children took PRECEDENCE over profits and promptly recalled the defective item from the stores.*

preceptor (pri-SEP-tur): a school principal, teacher, or instructor.

> *Our elementary school's PRECEPTOR was a stern man who handed out swift discipline to troublemakers.*

precipitous (pruh-SIP-uh-tuss): very steep, as a precipice; rushing away headlong.

> *The prospect of learning to drive a standard shift in this city of PRECIPITOUS hills is an intimidating one.*

precept (PREE-sept): a rule, order, or principle that sets up a standard guide for conduct.

> *I make it a personal PRECEPT never to ask my staff to do anything I would not be willing to do myself.*

precocious (pruh-KOE-shuss): pertaining to or reminiscent of one (particularly a child) who acts in a manner generally expected of an older person; ahead of fashions, times, or standards.

> *Charlie's PRECOCIOUS four-year-old, Willie, likes to walk into the den while we're drinking beer and watching football games and ask whether we can't think of a better way to spend our time.*

predestined (pre-DESS-tind): controlled by the fates; governed by higher powers and foreordained.

> *After his meeting with the fortune-teller, Jim honestly believed he was PREDESTINED to meet and marry a woman from Argentina.*

preeminent (pre-EM-ih-nunt): superior to others.

> *The young Stalin's plan was to reach a PREEMINENT position in the party hierarchy by any means necessary.*

preen (preen): to primp; to perfect one's appearance. Also: to take pride (in oneself or one's accomplishments).

The crew knew that the reason Barry arrived at the studio an hour before broadcast was so that he would have plenty of time to PREEN in front of the mirror before going on camera.

premise (PREM-iss): the idea or statement that stands as the base of a theory or argument; also, the conceit underlying the action of a work of fiction or drama.

The story's PREMISE—that all of us can win the lottery if we only play it enough times—is so farfetched as to be laughable, but the piece is not, alas, intended as a comedy.

prenatal (pre-NAY-tull): occurring before childbirth.

Dr. Ellis advised all her patients to follow a sound PRENATAL regimen that included a diet rich in protein, calcium, and iron.

preposterous (prih-POSS-tur-uss): so outlandish as to be unbelievable; incredible.

Your suggestion that we hold the board meeting in the park in order to enjoy the warm weather is simply PREPOSTEROUS, James.

prevalent (PREV-uh-lunt) occurring often; common.

Although a belief that some kind of conspiracy in President Kennedy's murder is certainly PREVALENT in public opinion these days, there is no consensus on the nature of that purported conspiracy.

primer (PRIM-ur): a basic, grade-school textbook.

For decades, the foundation of American schooling was the old-fashioned PRIMER, from which children studied subjects ranging from history to poetry to arithmetic.

principal (PRIN-sih-pul): first in importance. Also, as a noun: the main performer in a dramatic production; also, the head of an elementary or high school. (See, for comparison, the entry for *principle*.)

> *My PRINCIPAL objection to your plan is that it is completely unethical, but I might also add that it is not likely to yield any significant income for our company.*

principle (PRIN-sih-pul): a common truth or law; a standard of behavior. (See, for comparison, the entry for *principal*.)

> *Melanie's assertion that our former Congressman is an overweight graft artist without a single moral PRINCIPLE was out of line; he's lost a good deal of weight in recent months.*

prodigal (PROD-ih-gul): extravagant or wasteful; imprudent.

> *Helen's PRODIGAL spending habits were well known to the family, and were one of the main reasons they fought her bid to take over the business.*

prodigious (pro-DIDGE-uss): impressive in size, impact, or stature; amazing.

> *Clark's PRODIGIOUS collection of old movie posters led many of his friends to ask whether he had once owned a theatre.*

proffer (PROF-fur): to offer; to tender or volunteer (a thing); as a noun, a thing offered.

> *Colin PROFFERED his car as a means of getting to Florida for spring break, but as none of us knew how to drive a standard, we had to decline.*

profusion (pro-FYOOZH-un): an abundance or extravagance.

> *Jane's fiance insisted on sending her such a PROFUSION of flowers that she soon ran out of places to put them.*

proselytize (PROSS-ih-li-tize): to convert (a person) from one religion to another.

> *Thus it was that our main goal of PROSELYTIZING the natives was temporarily abandoned in favor of the more pressing and immediate object of surviving their raids on our settlement.*

prosthesis (pross-THEE-sis): an artificially constructed member meant to replace a damaged or missing part of the human body.

> *Several months after the accident, Greg was fitted for a PROSTHESIS for his lower left leg that would allow him to walk again.*

protean (PRO-te-un): versatile; changing form easily.

> *As further demonstration of his PROTEAN abilities as an actor, Ned agreed to appear in a six-week run of Henry IV, Part One, playing Falstaff and Hotspur on alternate nights.*

proximity (prok-SIM-ih-tee): close or near in time, location, or relation.

> *The PROXIMITY of my desk to Irma's meant that I would be subject to her endless, tedious stories about her crocheting classes.*

proxy (PROK-see): one given authority to act on behalf of another. Also, the permission one gives another to act in one's place.

> *As I didn't want to reschedule my next vacation, I named Donna as my PROXY for the next stockholder's meeting.*

psoriasis (suh-RIE-uh-suss): a chronic skin disease causing the skin to become covered with red patches and white scales.

Emmett treated his first bout of PSORIASIS by applying copious amounts of moisturizer, but it did no good.

pumice (PUM-iss): a lightweight volcanic rock used in powder form as a cleanser.

For three hours I scrubbed the basin with the pink, gritty PUMICE the guard had supplied, but I could not remove the orange blotches.

punctilio (pungk-TIL-ee-o): a fine point of etiquette.

"Don't use dessert forks during the main course, please," my grandmother intoned, reverting to one of her favorite PUNCTILIOS.

pundit (PUN-dit): an educated or authoritative person whose opinion is generally respected.

The political PUNDITS had all decreed that Truman would be defeated in a head-to-head contest with Governor Dewey, but the voters had other ideas.

pungent (PUN-junt): powerful or sharp (typically used with regard to odors or tastes).

That PUNGENT odor coming from the back of the refrigerator is what's left of the lasagna Chris made three months ago.

puny (PYOO-nee): very little; being small in stature or strength.

A brilliant but rather PUNY child, Jason often had to endure the taunts and abuse of the school bully.

purge (purj): to free (someone or something) of all that is perceived as bad; to take steps to cleanse or purify.

I tried to PURGE my system of the flu virus by drinking endless glasses of fruit juice, but I still ended up missing a week of work.

purvey (pur-VAY): to supply.

Beluga caviar, PURVEYED by a local gourmet shop, was set out for the guests on large silver trays.

pusillanimous (pyoo-sih-LAN-ih-muss): cowardly; profoundly lacking in noble qualities of courage and mettle.

The actor made a career of playing PUSILLANIMOUS types in movies and on television, but he was apparently a robust and vigorous man of action in real life.

pyromaniac (pye-roe-MAY-nee-ak): one who compulsively sets fires.

Police believe that the blaze is not the work of an arsonist out for commercial gain, as was initially suspected, but the art of a PYROMANIAC.

quaff (kwoff): to drink heavily; to engage in the robust intake of alcoholic beverages.

On his twenty-first birthday, Sean vowed, he would QUAFF at least one glass of beer at every tavern in the city.

quahog (KWAW-hog): an edible clam found off of the Atlantic coastline of North America.

Every summer Grandpa would take us to his beachhouse in Maine, where we'd fish and dig for QUAHOGS in the quiet hours before dawn.

quandary (KWON-duh-ree): a dilemma; a difficult or uncertain situation.

> *Alisha found herself in a real QUANDARY when she realized she'd asked two dates to the prom.*

quarantine (KWOR-un-teen): to set apart; to isolate from others in order to prevent the spread of disease.

> *An elementary knowledge of public health procedures would have led you to QUARANTINE this area immediately, Dr. Miller.*

quaver (KWAY-vur): to tremble, shake, or quiver.

> *Eddie's hand QUAVERED as he extended the box containing the diamond ring across the table toward Helene.*

quell (kwell): to subdue; to crush or extinguish; to overcome.

> *The police sought to QUELL the rioters by using tear gas, but due to equipment malfunctions were unable to do so.*

quid pro quo (kwid pro KWO): a thing given in return for something else; Latin: "something for something."

> *Ryan's acceptance of a $40,000 check in return for a written promise to vote in favor of the highway project, a staggeringly obvious QUID PRO QUO, led to his indictment.*

quiescent (kwee-ESS-unt): dormant; inactive.

> *The old piano that had once rung out triumph after triumph had been standing QUIESCENT in its oak-paneled room since the day of its master's death.*

quirk (kwurk): an idiosyncrasy; an odd behavioral or personality characteristic.

I hope you can overlook Mr. Johnson's QUIRK of using rough language with outside salespeople.

quisling (KWIZ-ling): one who betrays his or her own country and aids an invading one; particularly, an official who serves in a puppet government.

That the Vichy government in France was composed primarily of cowards, profiteers, and QUISLINGS is hardly open to dispute.

quizzical (KWIZ-ih-kul): puzzled.

Chris gave his boss a QUIZZICAL look upon being told he would not receive any pay for the next month.

rabble (RAB-ul): a mob; a rowdy crowd or disorderly group.

Flashing cameras recorded the journey of the accused as the police guided him through the RABBLE that had gathered on the courthouse steps.

rambunctious (ram-BUNK-shuss): difficult to manage or control; extremely boisterous.

We love to have Roman and Marlena over for dinner, but their three-year-old is so RAMBUNCTIOUS that no one gets to relax and enjoy the meal.

rampage (RAM-page): an instance reminiscent of frenzied violence; a destructive period of self-indulgent behavior.

"The tiniest mistake sends my boss on a RAMPAGE," the senior staffer moaned.

rampant (RAM-punt): widespread; unrestrained.

The obedience trainer told us that because we had allowed our dogs to run RAMPANT through our old apartment, we would have a hard time keeping them confined to one area of the new house.

rancor (RAN-kur): intense ill-will; bitter resentment.

Mike's RANCOR toward his ex-wife was so intense that the mere mention of her name was sometimes enough to send him into a tirade.

rapport (rah-PORE): a trusting and peaceful mutual relationship.

Although the Wilsons found their neighbors odd at first, the four soon developed a strong RAPPORT.

raucous (RAW-kuss): rowdy; boisterous; disorderly and wild. Also: harsh or grating to the ear.

My parents' fears that we would use their vacation as an opportunity to stage RAUCOUS parties in the den were not entirely without foundation.

raze (raze): to flatten, level, or demolish.

Despite our arguments that the building had significant historical value and should be restored, the planning board authorized its demolition; within a week of the meeting, it was RAZED.

recede (rih-SEED): to move back or away.

My brother is so sensitive about his RECEDING hairline that he's started wearing a hat whenever he goes out in public.

recidivism (rih-SID-ih-viz-um): repeated relapse into a past condition or behavior.

> *The rate of RECIDIVISM for inmates in this institution is woefully high, Warden.*

reciprocal (rih-SIP-ri-kul): given in return for something else; mutually negotiated.

> *Many economists feel that the U.S. economy cannot truly improve until the United States is able to negotiate a RECIPROCAL trade agreement with the Japanese.*

recrimination (rih-krim-ih-NAY-shun): an accusation made in response to an accusation; a countercharge.

> *Bo knew that divorce proceedings often degenerated into endless, bitter rounds of seemingly pointless RECRIMINATION.*

redoubtable (rih-DOUT-uh-bull): inspiring wonder or awe; worthy of respect.

> *The REDOUBTABLE Saint George mounted his charger and set off in search of his next dragon.*

redundant (rih-DUN-dunt): unnecessarily repetitious.

> *By the end of the lecture, Professor Smith's points began to seem a little REDUNDANT, and I gave up taking notes when she said for the third time, "And as I stated earlier . . . ."*

refulgent (rih-FUL-junt): radiant.

> *A REFULGENT smile crossed Anna's face when she learned that her loan had been approved.*

regale (rih-GALE): to entertain; to give delight. Also, to provide pleasure, particularly by means of food, spectacle, or the like.

In this film, although the millionaire REGALES the innocent country girl with beautiful gifts and a lavish week on the town, money isn't enough to win her heart in the end.

regurgitate (rih-GURJ-ih-tate): to vomit; to cast (something) back again.

Frankly, the prospect of working all night on the project made me want to REGURGITATE, but the deadline was near and it had to be met.

reiterate (re-IT-uh-rate): to restate or say again; to repeat.

Let me REITERATE: There will be no exception to the official policy on removing unauthorized recordings from the studio.

relapse (RE-laps): a return or slip back into an old condition, state, or mindset.

Mom warned me that I'd have a RELAPSE of the flu if I stood out in the cold watching the football game for three hours, and she was right.

relegate (REL-uh-gate): to assign or place in a position, often one of low prestige or power; to set out of sight; banish.

Although the press release described Lou's new position as a promotion, he and everyone else in the organization knew he was being RELEGATED to a less prominent spot in the hierarchy after the fiasco of the Darwin project.

relevant (REL-uh-vunt): pertaining to or having bearing, influence, or relation to the matter at hand.

> *The defense attorney argued vehemently—but in vain—that the accused's past history was not RELEVANT to the case.*

relish (REL-ish): to enjoy heartily; also, an instance of great enjoyment. (Also: a sweet pickle dish composed of various vegetables.)

> *On particularly difficult days, Barbara RELISHED a private fantasy of kicking Mr. Wilkins in the shins.*

remand (rih-MAND): to send back.

> *The judge REMANDED the case much more quickly than had been expected, issuing an unusually thorough set of instructions for the lower court to follow.*

reminisce (rem-uh-NISS): to recall the past; to remember; to have memories.

> *I used to like to sit on the porch swing with Grandma on those cool summer nights and listen to her REMINISCE about her childhood in Italy.*

remiss (rih-MISS): negligent; unreliable or careless in one's duties.

> *I hired Ted because he was my friend, but if he continues to be REMISS in his duties I'm afraid I'm going to have to let him go.*

remonstrate (rih-MON-strate): to protest, object, or offer disapproval; to offer objection or specific complaint.

> *Neighborhood parents packed the meeting to REMONSTRATE with the school committee for voting to close the local elementary school.*

remuneration (rih-myoon-uh-RAY-shun): something provided in exchange for goods or services; payment.

> *Fred was quite comfortable with the general idea of working in the automotive industry; it was the low level of REMUNERATION he couldn't get used to.*

renaissance (REN-uh-sonce): a rebirth or revival. Also (when capitalized) the period of artistic and cultural renewal in Europe that extended from, roughly, the fourteenth to seventeenth centuries; (when lower-case) a similar reawakening of dormant interests, spirits, or abilities.

> *Leonardo Da Vinci is recognized by most historians as the preeminent scientific and artistic genius of the RENAISSANCE.*

rendezvous (RON-day-voo): a meeting; especially, a secret meeting between lovers.

> *Claire knew that if her mother found out about her RENDEZVOUS with Elton, she would be grounded for at least a week.*

renowned (rih-NOWND): famous or well-known.

> *We were all thrilled to learn that a RENOWNED author of your caliber had agreed to teach at the university this semester, sir.*

repercussion (ree-per-KUSH-un): an echo; reverberation; also, the result of an action, often negative.

> *The REPERCUSSIONS of Ben's cheating were more severe than he had expected: a failing grade for the class and a two-week suspension.*

replica (REP-lih-kuh): a copy, imitation, or facsimile of an original.

> *While Steve was in Paris he bought a REPLICA of the Mona Lisa for his mother.*

repose (rih-POSE): an instance of resting after exercise or strain; also, tranquil rest reminiscent of eternal or heavenly ease.

> *We hiked in the Blue Hills from sunrise to sunset, stopping only for a brief REPOSE by the lake around midday.*

resilient (rih-ZIL-yunt): having the ability to survive; likely to rebound, particularly from hardship.

> *Although Rudy failed to make the team during his freshman year, he was RESILIENT and dedicated enough to earn a spot the next year.*

resonant (REZ-uh-nunt): pertaining to or reminiscent of a sound (often deep and pleasant) that echoes or continues.

> *The calm, RESONANT tone of the professor's voice was, after a night without sleep, very nearly enough to put me asleep.*

respite (RESS-pit): a reprieve; an instance of temporary relief.

> *Mark had worked on the book for six weeks straight without RESPITE.*

restaurateur (reh-stuh-ruh-TUR); a person who manages and owns a restaurant.

> *The Andersons had no one to complain to when they discovered their rude waiter was none other than the RESTAURATEUR himself.*

reticulate (rih-TIK-yoo-lit): like a net or network. Also, as a verb (rih-TIK-yoo-late): to cause to take the form of a network.

> *The maple leaf's fibers are RETICULATE in structure.*

retort (rih-TORT): to reply in a sharp, sometimes retaliatory fashion; (as a noun:) a biting reply.

> *"Well, if you're so smart, " Frank RETORTED, "why did you drop the ball on the five-yard line?"*

retraction (rih-TRAK-shun): a formal renunciation of statements considered or determined to be false or injurious to reputation.

> *After erroneously linking Mr. Vining to organized crime figures, the paper was forced to issue a front-page RETRACTION explaining and acknowledging its mistake.*

revelry (REV-ul-ree): uninhibited celebration.

> *Although Allan had a lot of work to do, he couldn't resist joining in the REVELRY that accompanied the office Christmas party.*

Rhode Island (rode EYE-lund): the thirteenth state of the United States.

> *The capital of RHODE ISLAND is Providence.*

rife (rife): widespread; commonly occurring.

> *Unimaginably poor sanitary conditions, RIFE in London at the time, were the chief cause of the sufferings of the plague years.*

riff (RIFF): in music, especially jazz and rock, a short melodic phrase repeated as background or used as a main theme.

> *Once the bass player started playing the insistent opening RIFF to "My Girl," people poured out onto the dance floor.*

riposte (rih-POAST): in fencing, the thrust made in response to an opponent's parry; also, a retaliatory remark or retort.

> *I thought Newman was good-natured enough to handle my jokes about his receding hairline, but his heated RIPOSTE about my weight problem indicated otherwise.*

roman à clef (ro-MON ah KLAY): a purportedly fictional work that only thinly veils the actual experiences of the author or of characters based on real personages.

> *Capote was ostracized by those in his circle when he published a devastating excerpt from a ROMAN À CLEF,* Unanswered Prayers, *that lampooned the frailties and indiscretions of the people who had been closest to him.*

rote (rote): routine or mechanical in fashion; repetitive.

> *The ROTE memorization of facts, long a staple of the public educational system, began to fall into disfavor in the late 1960s.*

roué (roo-AY): a licentious man; a libertine or lecher.

> *Although Ernest's dalliances might have been understandable when he was a young man, they were more difficult for his family to forgive in his later years, when he came to resemble nothing so much as a tired and lonely old ROUÉ.*

rube (ROOB): slang for an unsophisticated person; a bumpkin.

> *"Look at those RUBES over there," Charlie scoffed; "they wouldn't know a good restaurant if it smacked them in the face."*

rue (roo): to be sorrowful; to mourn or regret bitterly.

> *After spending prom night at home watching movies by herself, Susan began to RUE the day she had rejected Mark so cruelly.*

sacrilegious (sak-ruh-LIDJE-uss): profane; blasphemous toward something considered holy or sacred.

> *Some in the audience considered the director's decision to omit the famous "to be or not to be" speech nothing short of SACRILEGIOUS.*

saffron (SAFF-ron): a variety of crocus that blooms in the autumn. Also: a spice. Also: yellow-orange in color.

> *The September page of my calendar is my favorite: trees with leaves of red, orange, and gold, surrounded by a field of purple SAFFRON.*

sagacious (suh-GAY-shuss): perceptive; showing sound judgment.

> *Brian is the perfect candidate for chairman of the board; experienced, patient, and SAGACIOUS enough to help us counter the threat from our competitor.*

sake (SAH-kee): a wine-like Japanese beverage made with fermented rice.

> *When he returned from California, my father and I dined on sushi and drank warm SAKE at his favorite Japanese restaurant.*

salient (SAY-lee-unt): striking, obvious.

> *Let's not get bogged down in the details of the bonus plan; the SALIENT point is, we've provided our editors with a measurable financial incentive to do the very best acquisitions work they can.*

sallow (SAL-low): colorless; sickly-looking.

> *The SALLOW tone of Melanie's skin led us to wonder whether she was ill.*

salubrious (suh-LOOB-ree-uss): healthful; promoting or contributing to good health.

> *Working out at the health club was definitely a more SALUBRIOUS use of my spare time than sitting at home in front of the television eating potato chips.*

sanctimonious (sank-tih-MONE-ee-uss): hypocritical; two-faced, especially with regard to matters of morals or religion.

> *Despite his SANCTIMONIOUS brayings on issues of "family values," Reverend Wilton certainly seems to know his way around a certain part of town, according to the reporter who trailed him there last night.*

sanctum (SANK-tum): a holy, sacred place.

> *Brandon's small home office contained little more than a computer, an encyclopedia, and a few pieces of furniture, but it was in this unprepossessing SANCTUM that he wrote his Pulitzer Prize-winning play.*

sangfroid (san-FRWA): the state of being supremely composed or self-assured, especially in the face of adversity or danger.

I always marveled at Janie's SANGFROID before taking exams; I usually got so nervous I could hardly hold a pencil.

sangria (sang-GREE-uh): a cocktail of Mexican origin consisting of wine and fruit juices.

The cool cantina, with its seemingly endless supply of enchiladas and SANGRIA, was just what we needed after a long day of sightseeing in the hot Acapulco sun.

sanguinary (SANG-gwuh-nare-ee): marked by bloodshed.

They awoke the next morning to find that the battle had been won, but not without cost: it had been the most SANGUINARY encounter of the two-year conflict.

sans (sans): without.

On the MTV show "Unplugged," rock artists perform their songs SANS electric instruments and amplifiers.

sate (sate): to satisfy completely or to excess.

Our hunger for television SATED for the evening, we switched off the set and looked for a good book to read aloud.

satire (SA-tire): a humorous work employing sarcasm or irony in order to ridicule, expose, or make light of a person, institution, or practice.

I wonder how many of the young children now streaming to theaters to watch this cartoon are accompanied by adults who can appreciate its subtle SATIRE of consumer culture.

saunter (SON-tur): to walk leisurely or for pleasure.

> *On Sunday afternoons, Mr. Weeks would SAUNTER through Central Park gathering material for his short stories.*

savoir faire (SAV-whah FAIRE): tact or social skill.

> *I'm afraid Helen just doesn't have the SAVOIR FAIRE necessary to build coalitions in such a fractious organization.*

scalene (SKAY-leen): in geometry, having no two equal sides.

> *In geometry we learned about the six kinds of triangles: right angle, acute, isosceles, obtuse, equilateral, and SCALENE.*

scanty (SCAN-tee): insufficient; noticeably lacking.

> *The food at this restaurant is certainly good, but the portions are a little too SCANTY for the price we're paying.*

schadenfreude (SHAH-dun-froy-duh): an instance of rejoicing at the misfortune of another.

> *Wilson's conviction on perjury charges set off a festival of SCHADENFREUDE among his many conservative detractors.*

schism (SKIZ-um): a division; a break or rupture of relations, especially one due to ideological or political differences.

> *The SCHISM in the party over the issue of slavery reflected a division in the country itself.*

schizophrenia (skits-uh-FREEN-ee-uh): a mental condition that often causes sufferers to hallucinate, to be disoriented, and often to withdraw from society.

> *It is a common misconception that the term "SCHIZOPHRENIA" refers to the condition of multiple personalities.*

schlemiel (shluh-MEEL): an unlucky or awkward individual who can never seem to get the best of a situation.

> *My guess is, that used car salesman had Mike pegged for a SCHLEMIEL the second he stepped onto the lot.*

schlimazel (shluh-MOZ-ul): someone who endures constant bad luck.

> *Over the past year, Jonah's car was stolen, his house burned down, he lost his job, and he broke his leg—all of which earned him an impromptu "SCHLIMAZEL of the Year" award from his coworkers at the company party.*

schmaltzy (SHMALT-see): overly sentimental (especially with regard to music or art); tastelessly overdone.

> *Although Libby loved her great-grandfather, she found his SCHMALTZY taste in music hard to bear.*

scintilla (sin-TILL-uh): the smallest imaginable portion.

> *Your Honor, the prosecution's case, which is based entirely on hearsay, is unsupported by a SCINTILLA of hard evidence.*

scion (SIE-on): a person directly descended from a given line.

My professor told me my claim to be a SCION of William Shakespeare's line was totally at odds both with the existing genealogical information and with the quality of writing in my term paper.

scull (skull): a long oar used in the stern of a boat; also, a light racing rowboat. As a verb: to propel a boat with a scull.

Stewart loved to get up early in the morning and SCULL around the calm lake.

scurrilous (SKUR-ih-luss): offensive to civilized discourse; verbally abusive.

Because they were made on the floor of the Senate, the Senator's SCURRILOUS accusations against me were protected,but if he should dare to repeat them in another setting I will sue him for every penny he's worth.

seasonable (SEE-zun-uh-bull): timely; in keeping with or appropriate to the season. (See, for comparison, the entry for *seasonal*.)

In December, the outside of our building is done up in SEASONABLE green and red lights.

seasonal (SEE-zun-ul): happening as a result of regular and anticipated changes occurring at a specific time of the year.

Don't worry; that dramatic drop in sales for February is a SEASONAL dip experienced to one degree or another by everyone in our industry.

secede (sih-SEED): To withdraw officially and formally from an organization or union; to renounce one's membership.

> *After Lincoln's election to the presidency, the southern states, with South Carolina leading the way, began to SECEDE from the Union.*

seclude (sih-KLOOD): to hide or keep apart; to keep in isolation.

> *The two met in a woody, SECLUDED area of the estate to be sure their conversation would not be overheard.*

secular (SEK-yuh-lur): not religious in form or content; worldly.

> *Although the Cardinal had a long list of ecclesiastical issues to review with me, he began our interview with a few wholly SECULAR remarks on the poor fortunes of the Red Sox this year.*

sedentary (SED-un-tare-ee): involving the act of sitting; accustomed to a lack of movement or exercise.

> *Although I have nothing against watching television during the work week, I do like to engage in less SEDENTARY activities on weekends.*

sedition (sih-DISH—un): words or actions directed against public order; the incitement of disorder or rebellion.

> *The dictator's charges of SEDITION against his political opponents were met with skepticism by the international press.*

sedulous (SED-yuh-luss): done or crafted with skill, diligence, and care.

The teen's SEDULOUS labors at the desert site were rewarded by the discovery of triceratops bones in the third week of the dig.

segregate (SEG-ruh-gate): to separate or keep apart from others.

As the judge seemed doomed to have to point out for the rest of his life, his order affected only those school districts whose officials deliberately practiced SEGREGATION in violation of law—not segregation that was purely the result of existing demographic patterns.

segue (SEG-way): in music, to pass from one section to another; also, as a noun, any connective matter linking, for example, otherwise unrelated thoughts or observations.

Tomlin's mature routines, which featured random observations on the eccentricities of life with few or no SEGUES, were risky but always rewarding.

semantic (suh-MAN-tic): related to or having to do with the diverse levels of meaning accompanying words and symbols.

Whether we identify them as "streetwalkers" or "prostitutes," Mr. Mayor, is a matter of SEMANTICS; the fact is that the people plying their trade on our streets at night are reducing the quality of life in our town.

semaphore (SEM-uh-fore): a method of (usually seafaring) communication or signaling based on the positionings of the arms of a standing person or the similar positioning of flags (with one held in each hand).

> *Mark's attempt to render the complete works of Goethe in SEMAPHORE makes for a dedicated, if not exactly enthralling, piece of long-term performance art.*

sequential (sih-KWEN-shul): an order of arrangement or succession; one after another in arrangement.

> *The class graduation proceeded in SEQUENTIAL order from the beginning of the alphabet to the end, which Jane Zsilow found disheartening.*

serenity (suh-REN-ih-tee): peacefulness in outlook; a lack of agitation.

> *Although she had always been a whirlwind of activity while we were growing up, my sister Alice seems to be enjoying the SERENITY of convent life.*

serf (serf): a member of the lower feudal class bound to the land in medieval Europe; a slave.

> *At times, Rufus felt he was moored to his little computer like a SERF to his plot of land.*

seriocomic (seer-ee-oh-KOM-ik): having both serious and humorous characteristics.

> *Like many of today's successful dramatists, Erica employs SERIOCOMIC themes in her work.*

serriform (SAIR-uh-form): shaped like a saw-edge; having ridges reminiscent of saw-teeth.

> *The two SERRIFORM pieces fit together perfectly, making a solid joint.*

servile (SUR-vil): overly eager to serve; slavish.

> *Marion's uncharacteristically SERVILE demeanor can only mean one thing: He wants a raise.*

severance (SEV-uh-runce): a division; a breaking away, as of a relationship.

> *Bill was able to negotiate a handsome SEVERANCE package when he left the company.*

severity (suh-VARE-uh-tee): great force or concentration; harshness.

> *The SEVERITY of Milton's remarks about my proposal's deficiencies came as a shock to me; he had told me before the meeting that he liked the idea.*

shako (SHACK-oh): a stiff, tall piece of military headgear, resembling a fez with an upright plume.

> *The guard's SHAKO trembled as he advanced toward us angrily.*

shear (sheer): to clip or cut. (See, for comparison, the entry for *sheer*.)

> *I'm afraid I'm not much good at SHEARING sheep; I can't cut the fleece evenly.*

sheer (sheer): absolute; utter. Also: transparent. (See, for comparison, the entry for *shear*.)

> *To work on a project for twenty-four hours straight is SHEER madness, Roland.*

shogun (SHO-gun): before 1868, the commander of the Japanese military.

> *The SHOGUNS of ancient Japan are considered among the most notable strategists in military history.*

shun (shun): to keep away from or avoid.

Wade's parents thought he would be glad they had agreed to chaperone the school dance, and seemed surprised when he SHUNNED them for the entire evening.

shunt (SHUNT): to change the direction of; to divert.

When his proposal was dismissed after less than a minute of discussion, Mark felt more than ever that his ideas were being SHUNTED aside without due consideration.

singsong (SING-song): rendered chantingly or with a musical air; spoken in a manner reminiscent of singing.

Bert taunted Arthur with a SINGSONG recitation of his most embarrassing incidents at school.

sinuous (SIN-you-uss): curvy, winding; having many turns.

I always make sure to slow down on the SINUOUS road up to the cabin.

site (site): a place or spot. (See, for comparison, the entry for *cite*.)

We will build the new library and treasure hall on this SITE.

skepticism (SKEP-tih-siz-um): an instance of doubt or uncertainty.

Your SKEPTICISM that we will be able to finish the work on time is understandable, given our history of delivering material late.

skulk (skulk): to move about furtively or quietly.

After she lost her job, Lea SKULKED around the town at odd hours, hoping to avoid her former colleagues.

skullduggery (skull-DUG-uh-ree): dishonest actions; cheating.

> *Mike accused me of throwing copying my answers to the math quiz; I replied that I had never engaged in such SKULLDUGGERY, or at any rate had never been caught, which in my view amounted to much the same thing.*

slander (SLAN-dur) an untrue and malicious statement intended to damage the reputation of another. (As a legal term, "slander" refers to oral, rather than written or pictorial, defamation.)

> *If I hear any more of your SLANDERS against my father, Mr. Caen, you will be hearing from my attorney.*

sloe (SLO): a small fruit resembling a plum.

> *Many people like the taste of SLOE gin, but Jennifer prefers the traditional variety flavored with juniper berries.*

sluggish (SLUG-gish): lacking vitality or alertness; lethargic.

> *As the hours drew on, I pecked away at my keyboard dutifully; toward morning, however, I could tell that I was getting SLUGGISH.*

smarmy (SMAR-mee): insincerely earnest.

> *In between syrupy love songs, the SMARMY lounge singer repeatedly assured the crowd they were by far the best audience he'd ever performed for.*

snafu (sna-FOO): an egregious but common error.

> *Supposedly, the word "SNAFU" is an acronym of the phrase "Situation normal, all fouled up."*

snit (snit): an angry or nasty mood; an irritated state.

After his roommate spilled grape juice all over his favorite coat, Jay was in a SNIT for weeks.

sociopath (SO-see-uh-path): a person who, because of mental illness, lacks restraint or moral responsibility toward fellow members of society.

Although motion pictures and popular fiction have shown an unending fascination with serial killers, the fact is that such SOCIOPATHS are quite rare.

solipsistic (sawl-up-SIS-tik): believing that the self is the only reality.

It's difficult to achieve the give-and-take qualities of a good discussion with Sandy, whose arguments tend to be a little SOLIPSISTIC.

solstice (SOL-stiss): either of the two yearly times during which the sun is furthest from the celestial equator; the longest and shortest days of the year in the Northern Hemisphere. (The longest day, known as the summer solstice, occurs in June; the shortest day, or winter solstice, is in December.)

During the Roman winter SOLSTICE festival, known as Saturnalia, revelers would put candles on trees and hold massive celebrations intended to persuade the fading sunlight to return.

somber (SOM-ber): depressing; joyless.

The SOMBER expression on my boss's face before our meeting made me wonder whether the long-rumored layoff was finally to be ordered, but as it turned out he had simply slept poorly.

somnolent (SOM-nuh-lunt): tired, sleepy.

Having worked all night on the paper, Gaylord dragged himself into the lecture hall and spent the hour casting a well-meaning but SOMNOLENT gaze in the direction of his professor.

somnambulist (som-NAM-byoo-list): a person who walks during sleep.

My father, the most notorious SOMNAMBULIST in our family, once emptied out the contents of the refrigerator before proceeding back upstairs to bed.

sonorous (SON-uh-russ): deep or rich in sound; also, overblown or conceited in language.

The chairman's SONOROUS but mercifully brief remarks brought the long meeting to a close.

sophomoric (sof-uh-MORE-ik): immature; overbearing in a conceited or pretentious way; characteristic of one with little learning but convinced that he or she is brilliant.

Preston was intrigued by the fraternity's offer of fun and games, but I found their SOPHOMORIC initiation rituals and elitist attitudes tough to take.

soporific (sop-uh-RIF-ik): causing or likely to cause sleep or drowsiness; anything likely to induce sleep.

Rick's endless speech on the social habits of the grouse was a poor choice for after-dinner entertainment, but, judging by the reaction of the group, an excellent SOPORIFIC.

soprano (suh-PRAN-oh): the uppermost singing voice in boys and women.

Every woman in the a capella group had a good voice, but to me the tall SOPRANO in the blue sweater stood out as an exceptional musical talent.

South Carolina (south kare-uh-LINE-uh): the eighth state of the United States.

The capital of SOUTH CAROLINA is Columbia.

South Dakota (south duh-KO-tuh): the fortieth state of the United States.

The capital of SOUTH DAKOTA is Pierre.

spasmodic (spaz-MOD-ik): characteristic of a spasm; brief and fitful.

The regime's SPASMODIC attempts at reform had yet to bring prosperity to the nation's citizens.

spate (spayt): a sudden outpouring; a flood or deluge.

My request for a raise was greeted by a SPATE of hysterical laughter and occasionally obscene rantings from my boss, Mr. Walker.

spatial (SPAY-shull): of or pertaining to physical space.

The cover artist's use of varying widths of type leaves the viewer with an intriguing sense of SPATIAL disorientation.

spay (spay): to render (an animal) infertile by removing the ovaries.

After she had whelped three litters, Myron decided that it was about time to have Queenie SPAYED.

specious (SPEE-shuss): something that appears to be good or right, but upon closer examination is not; superficially convincing but unsound.

My opponent's arguments may seem sound at first hearing, but if you will grant me five uninterrupted minutes, Mr. Moderator, I will show them to be SPECIOUS.

spectral (SPEK-trul): reminiscent of ghosts or spirits; gruesome and otherwordly.

> *Scrooge's SPECTRAL visitors take different forms, but each is interested in the same thing: the redemption of the old man's heart.*

spiel (shpeel): a long, extravagant argument or speech designed to persuade.

> *I let the salesman recite his SPIEL just to be polite, but the guy impressed me so much I ended up buying a vacuum cleaner.*

spurn (spurn): to reject with disdain.

> *Ginger had thought of trying to locate the child she had given up for adoption fifteen years before, but she was afraid he would SPURN her attempts to see him.*

squall (skwall): a sudden, violent burst of wind often accompanied by snow or rain.

> *Although it wasn't snowing all that hard, we had to delay our trip because the SQUALLS made visibility too poor for safe driving on the hill's narrow roads.*

squalor (SKWAL-ur): the state or quality of being filthy.

> *My mother knew full well that my roommates were not the tidiest men in the world, but she still seemed shocked when confronted with the unrepentant SQUALOR of our apartment.*

staccato (stuh-KAH-toe): made up of abrupt, separate parts.

> *Suddenly we were awakened by STACCATO bursts of gunfire in the next street.*

staid (stayed): serious and dignified.

Bert's fluorescent pinstripes and huge bow tie were not at all what his new supervisor had in mind when he called for STAID attire.

stalactite (stuh-LACK-tite): an icicle-shaped deposit hanging from the top of a cavern, formed by drips of water containing calcium or other minerals.

STALACTITES hang from the tops of caves; an easy way to remember this is that the second half of the word begins with a "t" for "top."

stalagmite (stuh-LAG-mite): a deposit, typically found on a cave floor, formed from the drippings of a stalactite.

STALAGMITES are found at the bottoms of caves; an easy way to remember this is that the second half of the word begins with a "g" for "ground."

stalemate: (STALE-mate): in chess, a condition in which neither side is in checkmate and the game cannot proceed because no legal move can be made; also, any situation in which progress, movement, or negotiation has becomes impossible.

I thought I had beaten Joreth when I captured the knight he had left undefended, but he was such a strong player that he was able to maneuver a STALEMATE.

stanch (stanch): to stop a liquid's flow (usually said of the bleeding accompanying a wound).

Dr. Cooper tied a tourniquet around Mark's injured arm to STANCH the flow of blood.

stationary (STAY-shun-air-ee): unmoving; fixed in place. (See, for comparison, the entry for *stationery*.)

> *Although the cart was designed to be wheeled freely, a set of clamps could be engaged that would allow it to serve as a STATIONARY post for nurses' supplies.*

stationery (STAY-shun-air-ee): writing paper. (See, for comparison, the entry for *stationary*.)

> *Following her wedding, Amy had STATIONERY embossed with her married name.*

status quo (STAH-tus KWO): the existing state of affairs or condition.

> *Although Bill desperately wanted to get married, Melanie was more interested in preserving the STATUS QUO.*

staunch (stonch): firm in resolution or belief; fixed.

> *Mr. West, a STAUNCH conservative, believed that government waste was the main problem requiring attention in Washington.*

stigmatize (STIG-muh-tize): to mark as wicked or infamous.

> *Many people with AIDS find that coping with the physical trauma of their disease is only part of their difficulty; another part is being STIGMATIZED by others as somehow deserving of punishment.*

stilted (STILL-tud): stiff and formal ; rigid and unspontaneous in nature.

> *The letter was composed in such STILTED, elaborately correct language that Sergeant Ryan surmised it was written by someone whose native language was not English.*

stipend (STIE-pend): a periodic payment, such as a scholarship or other allowance; remuneration for a service.

> *A small monthly STIPEND from the Institute made it possible for Vernon to continue his biography of Yeats.*

stoke (stoke): to poke or feed (a fire); to supply with fuel.

> *My opponent's remarks are meant to STOKE the fires of intolerance, not help us learn to live with one another.*

stolid (STOL-id): unemotional; impassive.

> *The witness retained her STOLID, professional demeanor in the face of some intense cross-examination.*

stopgap (STOP-gap): a temporary expedient.

> *We knew that keeping Dad inside the house by suggesting he watch the football game while we mowed the lawn was nothing more than a STOPGAP; sooner or later he'd have to see the huge dent Billy put in the car.*

stringent (STRIN-junt): imposing strict standards, rigid.

> *It was very difficult for Bonnie to adhere to such a STRINGENT diet, but she managed to do it.*

stucco (STUCK-oh): a plaster or cement wall finish.

> *The real estate agent explained that STUCCO homes were very popular in this area of southern California.*

stultifying (STULL-tih-fie-ing): likely to stifle or cause to be futile or ineffective.

> *It was on a STULTIFYINGLY hot August day in Memphis, Tennessee, that the idea of scaling back my daily running routine first occurred to me.*

stupefy (STOO-puh-fie): to make numb with amazement; to stun into helplessness.

> *The prospect of working until the morning hours left me STUPEFIED, but there was no alternative.*

stymie (STIE-mee): to thwart; to prevent (another) from achieving a goal.

> *The reporter's attempts to get to the bottom of the scandal were STYMIED by the refusal of the principals to talk to him—either on or off the record.*

subliminal (sub-LIM-ih-nul): operating below the level of conscious perception.

> *The advertising industry has long been suspected of using SUBLIMINAL implants in advertisements for cigarettes and liquor, but scientists and industry insiders have always scoffed at the notion.*

subsequent (SUB-suh-kwunt): after; following in time.

> *The butler at first denied that he'd had anything to do with the murder, but the SUBSEQUENT testimony of three witnesses eventually convinced him to confess.*

subsistence (sub-SIST-unce): the means required to support one's existence.

> *Mr. Best, I've gone five years without a raise, and inflation has turned what was once a reasonable wage into a SUBSISTENCE-level compensation.*

substantiate (sub-STANT-chee-ate): to provide proof or evidence; to give validity to.

> *The soft-drink company sought to SUBSTANTIATE the claim that their soda was the best tasting by holding blind taste tests in shopping malls across the country.*

subterfuge (SUB-tur-fyoodge): a misleading ruse or cunning evasion; a strategic avoidance employing deceit.

Nick knew he would have to come up with a clever SUBTERFUGE to get out of going to another boring Sunday dinner at his grandparents' home.

succinct (suck-SINKT): brief; pithy; concise.

Norman preferred to say a SUCCINCT goodbye to his brother before getting into the cab, rather than engaging in a long, drawn-out scene at the train station.

succor (SUCK-ur): aid or assistance; relief.

Although she did not participate in the crime, Mrs. Helm was sentenced to five years in prison for giving SUCCOR to men she knew to be kidnappers.

suffrage (SUFF-rudge): the right to vote.

Today's apathetic voters (or, more precisely, nonvoters) seem to have little appreciation of how hard previous generations had to fight for the principle of universal SUFFRAGE.

sultry (SUL-tree): very hot and moist; characterized by heat. Also: likely to arouse passion or romance.

I passed the SULTRY summer evenings in a beach chair with a margarita in hand, staring out at the expanse of tropical ocean.

supplicate (SUP-lih-kate): to make a humble, sincere, and earnest request of someone.

The department heads decided their best bet was to assemble as a group in the president's office and SUPPLICATE her to approve the budget increases.

surcingle (SUR-sing-gul): a strap that holds a saddle or other apparatus on a domesticated animal.

The worn leather SURCINGLE snapped, and Dan was thrown from the galloping horse.

surly (SUR-lee): sullen; gruff; morose.

Shiela, in the SURLY mood that accompanies her every working morning since the divorce, barked that I had no right to ask her for the report that was due last week.

surmise (sur-MIZE): to guess; to come to a conclusion (often without strong evidence).

We SURMISED that Leanna had declined the invitation to Arthur's birthday party simply because she didn't want to buy him a gift.

surrealism (suh-REE-uh-liz-um): a twentieth-century movement in art and literature that emphasized the subconscious or irrational nature of perceived forms through the illogical placing and presentation of subject matter.

Dali's "The Persistence of Memory," which features the now-famous melting watches, was immediately hailed as a masterpiece of SURREALISM.

surveillance (sur-VAY-lunce): an instance of watching something closely, usually in a scrutinizing fashion.

The police set up SURVEILLANCE in the house across the street from the escaped con's girlfriend, as they were sure he would try to visit her.

sustenance (SUS-tuh-nunce): means of supporting life.

After the bombing, the city's hungry occupants wandered through nearby wooded areas in search of SUSTENANCE.

sward (swored): land covered with thick grass.

We decided that the large, flat SWARD would make an excellent location for a game of touch football.

swelter (SWEL-tur): to suffer from extreme heat.

Jasmine and I found ourselves lost in the middle of the jungle, SWELTERING in the tropical heat.

sybarite (SIB-er-ite): a person enamoured of luxury and pleasure.

Rodney lived the life of a SYBARITE, driving his Rolls-Royce around his summer cottage in Nice and wintering at his Virginia mansion.

sycophant (SIK-uh-funt): one who tries to gain favor by flattering excessively.

Any film star used to being surrounded by an entourage of SYCOPHANTS is likely to find it difficult to keep things in perspective when questioned by an unsympathetic journalist.

sylph (SILF): a slim, graceful girl or woman.

Although the fashion industry now considered her to be the most exotic SYLPH on the scene, the fashion model had thought herself clumsy and awkward as a teenager.

symbiotic (sim-bee-OTT-ik): characteristic of an intimate or mutually advantageous relationship, especially (in biology) one between dissimilar organisms.

In ocean life you often see SYMBIOTIC relationships between large and small fish, in which the smaller feed off of organisms existing on the larger, thereby keeping the larger fish clean and healthy.

symposium (sim-POSE-ee-um): a meeting for discussion; especially, a gathering of experts before an audience whose members may pose questions.

The SYMPOSIUM was a disaster; both professors arrived an hour late, after most of the audience had given up and left.

synchronize (SINK-ruh-nize): to cause something to take place at the exact same time (as another event); to cause to occur in unison.

As this is an operation requiring the utmost accuracy from all team members, I suggest we SYNCHRONIZE watches now before beginning our assignments.

synonym (SIN-uh-nim): a word with a meaning similar or identical to that of another word in a language.

"Masculine" and "male" are SYNONYMS.

synthesis (SIN-thuh-suss): a combination of elements to form a new whole.

The writer's latest book is an intriguing SYNTHESIS of classical Greek tragedy and cyberpunk elements.

taboo (tuh-BOO): anything deemed absolutely unacceptable or immoral by a social order. Also: forbidden or off-limits.

Anthropologists have found that incest is a universal TABOO in human culture.

tacit (TASS-it): implied; understood without being openly explained or expressed.

The men took their sergeant's harsh language toward Ned as TACIT approval of their own abusive behavior toward him.

tactile (TACK-tul): of or pertaining to the sense of touch.

At this stage, your baby's need for TACTILE stimulation is intense; she must be held, stroked, and cuddled regularly.

tai chi chuan (tie jee chwan): a martial art of China that emphasizes slow, meditative movements.

Each morning, I saw Erica in the park practicing the gentle, fluid movements she'd learned in our TAI CHI CHUAN class.

talisman (TAL-iss-mun): a lucky charm; an engraved object believed to possess occult powers.

Justin was all set for the big game until he reached into his pocket and found that his TALISMAN—a small piece of stone from the shores of Ireland, given to him by his mother—was missing.

talkathon (TALK-uh-thon): an extended speech or discourse, especially one featuring excessive posturing.

I was told that this meeting was meant to explore the pros and cons of locating the waste site near our town, but I see we've moved toward a TALKATHON on the long-term benefits of the nuclear power industry.

tam-o'-shanter (TAM-o-shan-ter): a floppy Scottish hat with a tight headband.

Angus MacGregor, a man fiercely proud of his heritage, usually took the opportunity of a company picnic to don a kilt and TAM-O'-SHANTER and play his bagpipe.

tangelo (TAN-juh-lo): a kind of citrus fruit; hybrid of a tangerine and a grapefruit.

The corner fruit market specialized in stocking the more exotic fruits and vegetables, and for most of the year was the only place in town where one could regularly purchase TANGELOS.

tangential (tan-JEN-chull): divergent or digressive; only slightly connected (to a more important matter).

After reviewing the financial outlook for the coming year, the chairman closed the meeting with a few TANGENTIAL remarks on some new software the accounting department would be purchasing.

Taoism (DOW-is-um): a system of philosophy identified with the sage Lao-Tzu, and embodied most notably in his work *Tao-te-ching*, that holds that life lived simply and in accordance with natural laws and events is most in keeping with the Tao, or way, that underlies all existence.

Scholars may debate the fine points of a rational understanding of TAOISM, but a true practitioner probably expresses it best when she gracefully and thankfully accepts a proffered cup of tea.

taphephobia (taff-uh-FOE-bee-uh): the abnormal fear of being buried alive.

After seeing the final scene of that horror film, The Grave Claims Its Own, I couldn't sleep, and I had an inkling of what it must be like to suffer from TAPHEPHOBIA.

tarantella (tar-un-TELL-ah): a spirited Italian dance in 6/8 time.

Al, a dedicated foxtrotter, had a tough time dealing with his new wife's seemingly endless fascination with the TARANTELLA.

taut (taut): tight; firm.

This toy telephone will not work unless you pull the tin cans far enough apart to make the string TAUT.

tawdry (TODD-ree): cheap and tasteless; also, ostentatious and gaudy.

Although many in the publishing world considered the actress's tell-all book to be a sleazy foray into the TAWDRIEST kind of name-dropping, there were few who didn't envy its sales totals.

telegenic (tell-uh-JEN-ic): likely to make a good appearance on television.

When he's not doing his newscast, he's awkward and withdrawn, but once the camera is on, Lenny comes across as appealing, confident, and incredibly TELEGENIC.

tempera (TEM-pur-uh): a paint medium popularized during the Renaissance, generally composed of egg, oil, water, and pigment.

Raphael's early TEMPERA works have disintegrated badly over the centuries and are in need of restoration.

temperance (TEM-puh-runce): self-restraint; moderation; specifically, the act of abstaining from consuming alcohol or other intoxicating substances.

Although Mr. Bedford had been a model of TEMPERANCE for most of his adult life, he relented when I pleaded with him to try some of the punch we had made for the party.

tempestuous (tem-PESS-choo-uss): stormy, violent.

Lear's own rage and madness, far more than any artificial theatrical storm effects, are the truly TEMPESTUOUS elements of these scenes.

tempo (TEM-po): the speed or pace of something (particularly, of music).

> *Our aerobics instructor will only play music with a fast TEMPO and a strong beat, although there are times, generally after a hard day at work, when I feel like introducing her to the wonders of Mantovani.*

temporal (TEM-puh-rul): pertaining to or limited by time; characteristic of worldly (rather than celestial or heavenly) endeavor.

> *My father believed that TEMPORAL joys and sorrows were of little consequence in the grand scheme of things.*

tendril (TEN-drull): the small, coiling organ of a climbing plant, which encircles another object and thereby helps to support the plant's weight.

> *Even after the ivy was removed from the side of the old administration building, many of its TENDRILS remained firmly attached to the brickwork.*

Tennessee (ten-uh-SEE): the sixteenth state of the United States.

> *The capital of TENNESSEE is Nashville.*

tentative (TEN-tuh-tiv): given to or showing hesitation; lacking in resolution or consistency.

> *The parents were able to capture their child's first TENTATIVE steps on videotape.*

tepid (TEP-id): lukewarm in temperature; also, unenthusiastic.

> *Although he expected a loud and long ovation from the crowd in appreciation of his work, the playwright had to make do with a few pockets of TEPID applause and a low buzzing sound distinctly reminiscent of snoring.*

terrestrial (tuh-RESS-tree-ul): of or pertaining to the earth, or to life on earth.

Although life on a space station is interesting to read about, I still believe I'd be most comfortable in a TERRESTRIAL setting.

terse (turce): pithy; brief; concise.

Although I tried to pump Jim for information about his new girlfriend, his TERSE answers were a polite way of letting me know it was none of my business.

Texas (TEX-us): the twenty-eighth state of the United States.

The capital of TEXAS is Austin.

than (than *or* then): a conjunction used to introduce the second element of an unequal comparison. (See, for comparison, the entry for *then*.)

Bert is shorter THAN Velma is.

then (then): at that time. (See, for comparison, the entry for *than*.)

You should have known me back THEN!

their (thare): belonging to that group. (See, for comparison, the entries for *there* and *they're*.)

Many celebrities zealously guard THEIR privacy.

there (thare): in that place. (See, for comparison, the entries for *their* and *they're*.)

Although I've always wanted to visit Barcelona, I've never found the time or money I needed to vacation THERE.

they're (thare): they are. (See, for comparison, the entries for *their* and *there*.)

> *Mom and Dad just told me that THEY'RE planning to renovate the dining room.*

threshold (THRESH-old) an entranceway; a piece of stone or wood positioned under a doorway; also, the beginning or initiation of anything.

> *Those who were present for the final meeting agreed afterward that the countries had reached a new THRESHOLD in trade relations.*

throng (throng): a large crowd.

> *As the desperate editor stood on the tenth-floor ledge, a THRONG of spectators gathered on the street below.*

tiered (teerd): constructed or arranged in layers or levels.

> *In talking to bakeries about a wedding cake for my daughter, I was flabbergasted to learn that some of the elaborate TIERED cakes cost over a thousand dollars.*

timbre (TAM-bur): a quality of sound, usually musical, determined by its overtones; a distinctive quality or tone.

> *I feel that the haunting TIMBRE of the oboe, when played by a master, is more moving than that of any other musical instrument.*

tint (tint): a color or a degree of a color; a slight variation in shade. As a verb: to add or alter color, generally in a subtle way.

> *My mother was aghast when my sister Cassandra came back from her first semester at college with her golden-blonde-hair TINTED a pale orange.*

titanic (tie-TAN-ic): of enormous strength, influence or size.

The TITANIC explosion in the movie's final scene required several hundred pounds of dynamite and was filmed from eleven different angles.

torpid (TORE-pid): sluggish; inactive; reminiscent of an in hibernation.

My sister Helen was always involved in torrid romances; my boyfriends were invariably TORPID and uninteresting.

torque (tork): in mechanics, the force that causes twisting or rotation in a body.

The screwdriver was too small to generate enough TORQUE for the job.

tortuous (TORE-choo-uss): winding; full of twists and turns,

Drive safely; the road leading from the center of town up the side of the mountain is a TORTUOUS one.

totalitarian: (toe-tahl-ih-TARE-ee-un): characteristic of a system of government in which political power is highly centralized and in which authorities tolerate no dissent, punishing efforts at pluralistic discourse; of or pertaining to a governmental system that controls or dictates many aspects of life.

Although the worldwide fall of Communism has been widely discussed, several of its familiar TOTALITARIAN governments—notably those of China and North Korea—are still alive and kicking.

totem (TOTE-um): an animal, plant, or other natural object believed to be an ancestor of a tribe of peoples; a representation of such an object.

The tribe had an impressive collection of carved wooden TOTEMS.

totter (TOT-tur): to walk or move with unsteady steps; to sway at ground level.

The sight of Mr. Bass TOTTERING home from another night at Mulvaney's Pub was enough to make a teetotaler out of anyone.

tousle (TAU-zul): to muss up or dishevel.

Lynne admired the model's TOUSLED hair, but she knew that what looked sexy on a long, elegant face like that would look like an accident with a blender on her.

traduce (truh-DOOCE): to slander or defame; to speak falsely of or with malice toward (a person).

I was flabbergasted to learn that your campaign has tried to TRADUCE my character by offering cash payments to my ex-wife in return for her stories about me.

tragedian (truh-JEE-dee-un): an actor noted for performing tragic parts.

Richard Burbage was the premier TRAGEDIAN of the Elizabethan era.

traitorous (TRAY-tur-uss): reminiscent of or pertaining to a traitor; perfidious.

The third chapter of the book covered Benedict Arnold's TRAITOROUS acts and his eventual exposure as a British agent.

trajectory (truh-JEK-tuh-ree): the curving path followed by a projectile in flight.

> *The bullet's TRAJECTORY from the warehouse window would be completely consistent with the injury suffered by the victim, Your Honor.*

tranquillity (tran-KWIL-ih-tee): peacefulness; the state of being undisturbed.

> *After all the insanity of the deadline week, I was looking forward to the TRANQUILLITY of my annual vacation in Vienna.*

transcend (tran-SEND): to rise above common levels.

> *The young violinist's performance at the recital TRANSCENDED all of his teacher's expectations.*

transgress (trans-GRESS): to violate a principle or moral law.

> *After having TRANSGRESSED once, an agonized Henry knew he would never violate the club's rules again.*

transient (TRAN-zee-unt): existing only temporarily; brief; fleeting; transitory.

> *With seven children to care for, my wife and I knew that tranquility in the house was a TRANSIENT thing.*

transition (tran-ZISH-un): a change; a passage from one state or form to another.

> *Mark made the TRANSITION from actor to director with relative ease.*

transmogrify (trance-MOG-rih-fy): to change into a different shape or form.

Drink this and I promise you you'll be
TRANSMOGRIFIED into a poet for the ages.

transubstantiation (tran-sub-stan-shee-AY-shun): the theology that the bread and wine of the Eucharist became the actual body and blood of Jesus Christ, while retaining their original appearance.

The doctrine of TRANSUBSTANTIATION became a
main focus of disagreement between Protestants and
Catholics during the Reformation.

transvestism (tranz-VEST-iz-um): the act or practice of dressing for pleasure and gratification in the clothing of the opposite sex; especially, the practice of men dressing in women's garments.

Milton Berle's televised drag humor had far more to do
with his willingness to do anything for a laugh than with
any TRANSVESTISM on the comedian's part.

traumatize (TRAW-muh-tize): to cause to undergo mental or physical distress.

Many of the patients in the ward had been
TRAUMATIZED over the years by abusive staff.

treacle (TREE-kul): overly contrived sentiment; unrestrained mawkishness.

The movie's plot, which concerned a little blind girl's
search for her puppy, represented perhaps the most
unapologetic TREACLE of the year.

tremolo (TREMM-uh-lo): a quality of musical sound marked by rapid repetition of one or two notes.

The pianist played extravagantly, adding embellishments and trills of TREMOLO far too often for my taste.

trenchant (TREN-chunt): incisive and discerning.

Mort's TRENCHANT observations on Scorsese's films were a welcome addition to our discussion of major American directors.

triage (TREE-ozh): the procedure of prioritizing victims (of a battle or accident, for instance) to determine which will receive medical care first; of or pertaining to this procedure.

Nurse Victoria's single day in the TRIAGE unit of the mobile hospital left her so exhausted that she found herself wondering how the others worked there day after day.

trigamy (TRIG-uh-mee): the condition of being married to three husbands or three wives simultaneously.

As a result of two identical filing errors on the part of the county clerk in the years before her third marriage, Beth learned to her dismay that she was, technically at least, guilty of TRIGAMY.

trimester (try-MESS-tur): a period spanning three months.

For Beth, as for most women, the last few weeks of the final TRIMESTER of pregnancy was a challenging time.

tripartite (try-PAR-tite): consisting of three elements; involving three participants.

The TRIPARTITE trade agreement was signed by representatives of Canada, Mexico, and the United States.

trochee (TROE-kee): in poetry, a metrical element consisting of a two-syllable unit, the first stressed and the second unstressed.

The word "given" is a TROCHEE.

troika (TROY-kuh): a group of three individuals acting in concert to exert authority.

The photos he took at the historic conference included a memorable image of the victorious TROIKA: Churchill, Stalin, and Roosevelt.

trompe l'oeil (tromp LAY): an instance of visual trickery, as, for instance, an optical illusion giving the impression of three dimensions in a two-dimensional artistic medium.

The painter specialized in TROMPE L'OEIL murals that often fooled passersby into thinking they were walking toward a storefront.

trooper (TROO-pur): a military or police officer. (See, for comparison, the entry for *trouper*.)

I tried to talk my way out of the speeding ticket, but the TROOPER wouldn't hear any of it.

troubadour (TROO-buh-dore): a traveling medieval poet and singer; also, any wandering singer or minstrel.

After college, Ivan fancied himself something of a TROUBADOUR, and wandered from town to town in search of a coffeehouse willing to let him play.

trouper (TROO-pur): an actor, especially a veteran performer who is able to come through no matter what; also, any person who is remarkably dependable. (See, for comparison, the entry for *trooper*.)

Nancy drove through a snowstorm to man the desk on Saturday—what a TROUPER!

truculent (TRUCK-yuh-lunt): inclined toward conflict; eager to fight.

I had a run-in with a rather TRUCULENT sales clerk, who insisted, despite my receipt, that I had not bought the defective blender at his store.

truckle (TRUCK-le): to yield lamely or obsequiously.

I begged you not to TRUCKLE to that real estate agent's outrageous demands, but you wouldn't listen.

trumpery (TRUMP-uh-ree): worthless stuff; a thing or things without value; nonsense.

Mark's paper, composed between 3:00 and 6:00 a.m. on the day it was due, used complicated language to disguise its poor construction, but the instructor had seen such TRUMPERY often enough to recognize it instantly.

truncate (TRUN-kate): to shorten by cutting (a segment).

The director left the long passage about the "willow that grows aslant the brook" intact, but decided to TRUNCATE an earlier scene that had something to do with Hecuba.

tumescent (too-MESS-unt): swollen or beginning to swell.

The yellowjacket stung Rhoda on the thumb, leaving a TUMESCENT welt she felt compelled to show everyone in the office.

tundra (TUN-druh): a treeless arctic plain.

For days the members of the search team trekked through the frigid TUNDRA, but they at last they had to abandon the expedition without locating any survivors.

244

turncoat (TURN-kote): one who reverses sides in a conflict or changes principles easily.

At the risk of being labeled a TURNCOAT, I've decided to support your candidacy—even though you're a Democrat.

tutorial (too-TORE-ee-ul): a software program offering step-by-step instruction and demonstration in the use of another program; a component of a software program that offers instruction in the main program's use. Also: of or pertaining to tutors.

The manual that came with the software was woefully inadequate, but, fortunately, the program featured an excellent TUTORIAL.

tyranny (TEER-uh-nee): the abusive and unrestrained exercise of power.

Paine's bold arguments against the TYRANNY of George III made Common Sense *powerful reading.*

ubiquity (yoo-BIK-wih-tee): the quality of being (or of seeming to be) everywhere.

The UBIQUITY of that song, which you know I can't stand, is really beginning to get on my nerves.

ulterior (ul-TEER-ee-ur): being beyond what is obvious or put forth; lying beyond a recognized boundary.

I flatly reject the notion that my proposal to your daughter is occasioned by any ULTERIOR motive, sir.

ultimo (ul-TEE-mo): of or in the calendar month preceding the current one.

On the 23rd ULTIMO, I was informed by counsel that an indictment would be forthcoming.

ultrasaurus (ul-truh-SORE-us): a recently discovered species of dinosaur that is believed to have stood five stories high.

A dinosaur that would make a T. rex look like a pipsqueak may seem a farfetched notion, but scientists are now certain that the ULTRASAURUS was such a creature.

ululate (UL-yuh-late): to howl.

Late at night, Bert sometimes thought he heart faint sounds of the old house's former occupants ULULATING plaintively, as if imprisoned there.

umlaut (OOM-laut): a symbol (ü) used, especially in German, to indicate special pronunciation of vowels.

The German sportswriters in town for the race were unhappy with the typewriters we had provided, as they did not have UMLAUTS.

unanimity (yoo-nuh-NIM-ih-tee): agreement without dissent.

I was genuinely surprised at the UNANIMITY with which my proposal was accepted by the board.

unassuming (un-uh-SOOM-ing): modest; humble.

Sam is the UNASSUMING type who refuses to take credit after a job well done, preferring to cite the contributions of others.

unbecoming (un-bee-KUM-ing): unseemly; likely to detract from one's reputation or character.

I think your use of street language during the confirmation hearing was most UNBECOMING, George.

unblinking (un-BLINGK-ing): not displaying emotion or response. Also: unwavering in devotion.

Victor's UNBLINKING reaction to the judge's sentence left observers with no further insights on the motives that led him to commit the crime.

uncalled-for (un-KALD-for): improper or unjustified; also, superfluous.

That reference to my father's bankruptcy was UNCALLED-FOR, Senator.

uncanny (un-CAN-ee): strange; mysterious or otherwordly.

Greg's shooting ability is UNCANNY; I've seen him sink twenty foul shots in a row.

unceremonious (un-sare-uh-MONE-ee-uss): rude or abrupt; tactlessly hasty; inappropriate.

June made an UNCEREMONIOUS exit just as the chairman was beginning his remarks on the Fentworth project.

unconscionable (un-KONSH-un-uh-bul): lacking in principles our conscience; beyond any reasonable boundary.

Your decision to destroy those letters without attempting to get permission from the poet's widow was UNCONSCIONABLE.

uncouth (un-KOOTH): crude, without manners, unrefined.

Carl had an unfortunate way of belching loudly in public places, guessing (accurately and loudly) whether or not someone he just met had undergone plastic surgery, and otherwise acting in an UNCOUTH manner in front of strangers.

247

unctuous (UNK-choo-us): oily; falsely and exaggeratedly earnest; unpleasantly smooth.

An UNCTUOUS salesman glided across the lot and shook us both by the hand, telling us what a pleasure it was to meet such intelligent and discriminating customers.

underdog (UN-dur-dog): a person or entity expected to fail or to fare poorly.

San Diego, a decided UNDERDOG, somehow managed to pull out a win against the division-leading Miami team.

underhanded (UN-dur-hand): devious or deceitful in nature; not open, but crafty.

Who knows what UNDERHANDED means were used to turn the decision in Milton's favor?

undermine (UN-dur-mine): to defeat or destroy, as by sabotage.

Little did I know that Wells was UNDERMINING my efforts to win a contract for the project.

underwhelm (un-dur-HWELM): to fail to impress or excite. (Informal.)

After all the hype money could buy, the play opened to a wave of reviews written by unanimously UNDERWHELMED critics.

underwrite (UN-dur-rite): to support as by subsidy. Also, to support in full as though undertaking (a risk or venture) oneself.

A group of philanthropists UNDERWRITES our drama department's annual playwriting competition.

undisposed (un-dis-POZED): not inclined; not favoring.

Jim was not crazy about having to find a job, but he was also UNDISPOSED to letting his children go hungry.

unequaled (un-EE-kwuld): unmatched; without serious competition.

The salesman bragged of the car's "UNEQUALED level of trouble-free performance," but it broke down within two weeks of the time we bought it.

unequivocal (un-ee-KWIV-uh-kul): unambiguous; unadorned; blatant or obvious in expression.

My response to your suggestion that we lie to the judge is an UNEQUIVOCAL one: absolutely not.

unfaltering (un-FALL-tur-ing): unwavering; steadfast.

Frank's UNFALTERING composure on the witness stand, even under intense cross-examination, impressed us all.

ungainly (un-GANE-lee): graceless.

Wilma, who had always thought of herself as UNGAINLY, was surprised at the ease with which she and Clive moved across the dance floor.

ungrammatical (un-gruh-MAT-ih-kul): in violation of grammatical rules.

Fred's use of such UNGRAMMATICAL sentences as "Him and me want to talk at you" didn't score him any points with the college president.

unguent (UNG-gwunt): a locally applied ointment or salve.

In treating poison ivy, calamine lotion or some similar UNGUENT is usually recommended.

unicameral (yoo-nih-KAM-uh-rul): featuring a single chamber or body.

The new constitution provides for a UNICAMERAL legislature, rather than an upper and lower house.

unimpeachable (un-im-PEECH-uh-bul): exemplary; beyond reproach or suspicion.

My alibi for the night in question comes from an UNIMPEACHABLE source, Sergeant Miller; I was helping Father White at the homeless shelter.

unique (yoo-NEEK): singular; alone in a particular class.

Professor Watson would always scold me when I described something as "very UNIQUE," as something that is UNIQUE is by definition unparalleled, and therefore cannot be modified with a word like very.

unkempt (un-KEMPT): disheveled or messy; lacking care in aspect or look.

The witness's story was believable, but the defendant's lawyer worried about his UNKEMPT appearance.

unmitigated (un-MIH-tih-gay-tud); complete and without exception; unalloyed; sheer or outright.

Ron, who had worked on his article for six months, read the acceptance letter from the New Yorker with UNMITIGATED joy.

unobtrusive (un-ub-TROO-siv): not easily seen or noticed; not showy in nature.

The guards dressed in civilian clothes, taking seriously the pop star's request that his security detail be as UNOBTRUSIVE as possible.

unprecedented (un-PRESS-uh-dent-ud): new; unparalleled; not having been done before.

The studio granted Lewisohn UNPRECEDENTED access to the group's session tapes and related recording materials.

unremitting (un-ruh-MITT-ing): persistent; relentless.

An UNREMITTING rain spoiled our plans for a picnic.

unsavory (un-SAY-vuh-ree): likely to give social or moral offense. Also: unpleasant or distasteful.

I have no patience for biographers who concern themselves only with the number of UNSAVORY episodes they can uncover.

unseemly (un-SEEM-ly): inappropriate; unbecoming.

The family felt that Bill's presence at the memorial service would have been UNSEEMLY, as he had been my sister-in-law's bitterest business rival.

untenable (un-TEN-uh-bull): impossible; unsupportable.

The paper's central thesis, that Hamlet is a transvestite, is UNTENABLE to say the least.

untold (un-TOLD): not counted. Also: not revealed.

Greg used UNTOLD pads of paper in constructing the first draft of his epic.

unwarranted: (un-WORE-un-tud): groundless; lacking factual basis.

The defense will prove each and every one of these UNWARRANTED accusations to be false, Your Honor.

unwieldy (un-WEELD-ee): hard to handle or manage.

> *The deliveryman had a tough time getting that UNWIELDY package to our front door.*

unwitting (un-WIT-ting): unaware; unintentional. Also: unintended.

> *Greg was shocked to learn that he had been the UNWITTING stooge of a foreign espionage organization.*

upheaval (up-HEE-vul): a sudden, violent change.

> *Given the sense of UPHEAVAL in the department after the director's resignation, it's not too surprising that productivity has fallen.*

uprear (up-REER): to lift or raise up.

> *At the sound of the siren, our dog UPREARED her head and howled.*

upshot (UP-shot): a result or outcome.

> *The UPSHOT of Senator Green's poor performance in the debate is that his poll numbers have slipped by twenty percent.*

upside (UP-side): the positive aspect of a situation; particularly, the potential profit in a business proposal.

> *The UPSIDE of investing in the Russian company was considerable, but there were considerable risks as well.*

upthrust (UP-thrust): a quick, strong upward movement in the national economy or in the stock market.

> *This financial writer feels that the current UPTHRUST in the market cannot be sustained.*

urbane (ur-BANE): suave; sophisticated; debonair.

Clive, Linda's URBANE English cousin, was pleasant company for us all during his stay here.

usurious (yoo-ZHOOR-ee-us): charging excessive interest on money loaned; characterized by usury.

The rates we agreed to when we bought the house seem positively USURIOUS by today's standards.

Utah (YOO-tah): the forty-fifth state of the United States.

The capital of UTAH is Salt Lake City.

uxoricide (uk-SOR-ih-side): the crime of murdering one's wife.

Eventually, the defendant was acquitted of UXORICIDE; his wife's death was ruled a suicide.

uxorious (uk-SORE-ee-us): submissive or doting towards one's wife.

Although Grandpa makes a show of rebellion against Grandma's strictures every now and then for our sake, he's as UXORIOUS as they come.

vacuity (va-KYOO-ih-tee): empty; without content.

Staring out at the VACUITY of the Atlantic, Stan forgot for a moment the hazards of the journey ahead.

vagabond (VAG-uh-bond): leading the life of a person who has no home; transient.

Ivan's VAGABOND existence was not easy, but he was inured to it.

vainglorious (vane-GLORE-ee-uss): given to self-absorption; inclined to view oneself excessively or too highly.

Although some are entranced by Anais Nin's diaries, they always struck me as the narcissistic, VAINGLORIOUS observations of a woman totally unable to look beyond herself.

valedictory (val-uh-DIK-tuh-ree): saying farewell; of or pertaining to departing.

Karen was selected to give her class's VALEDICTORY address.

valiant (VAL-yunt): courageous, bold; brave.

I made a VALIANT effort to complete the project by the deadline, but in the end I had to get an extension from my boss.

valise (vuh-LEECE): a small piece of luggage; a carry-on bag.

The stewardess asked me to stow my VALISE in the overhead cabin.

vamoose (vah-MOOSE): to depart in haste; to leave hurriedly.

We've got a full day of travel ahead of us; let's VAMOOSE.

vanquish (VAN-kwish): to defeat as in combat.

Having VANQUISHED the enemy, the general returned victorious to his native land.

vapid (VA-pid): insipid; flat, dull, or lifeless.

The movie's scenery was appealing, but its VAPID characters made it hard for one to care about what was going on.

variorum (var-ee-OR-ee-um): a version of a literary work that may contain several different versions of the work as well as notes and criticism.

For the introductory course on Chaucer, we were required to purchase an unabridged VARIORUM edition of The Canterbury Tales.

vaticide (VAT-uh-side): the act of murdering a prophet.

Tom took the reviewer's negative article on his religious poetry as an act tantamount to VATICIDE.

vegan (VEH-jun): a person who eats only vegetables, fruits, and grains and no animal products whatsoever.

A VEGAN since college, Wanda had a hard time finding restaurants that offered entrees she could eat.

venal (VEE-nul): corruptible or excessively devoted to selfish interests (as opposed to public interests); susceptible to bribes. (See, for comparison, the entry for *venial*.)

The problem with politics by scandal, of course, is that it eventually leaves voters with the impression that all officeholders, regardless of ideology or experience, are VENAL, contemptible scalawags.

vendetta (ven-DET-uh): a bitter feud or grudge.

Mark's arguments against my proposed project had less to do with its merits than with the VENDETTA he has held against me since I was hired for the job he wanted.

255

veneer (vuh-NEER): a thin surface layer; a coating; a superficial surface or deceptive appearance.

> *Though it was not readily apparent to those who hadn't seen the supervisor in action, his VENEER of calm and approachability masked the temper and tolerance of a three-year-old.*

venerable (VEN-er-uh-bul): commanding reverence; sacred.

> *"Ladies and gentlemen," Bob intoned, "it is my privilege to introduce tonight's guest of honor, the VENERABLE Dr. Mildred Flint."*

venial (VEE-nee-ul): forgivable; excusable. (See, for comparison, the entry for *venal*.)

> *Mom told us that occasionally missing curfew was only a VENIAL offense, but lying to her about why we'd missed it was not.*

veracious (vuh-RAY-shuss): honest; truthful.

> *Your Honor, I ask that the defense's assertion that none of the prosecution's witnesses are VERACIOUS be stricken from the record.*

verification (veh-rih-fih-KAY-shun): something that confirms.

> *I could find no VERIFICATION of the author's claim that he had met with Hemingway in the early twenties.*

vermilion (vur-MILL-yun): scarlet red; bright red.

> *In her trademark VERMILION pantsuit, Carrie really stood out in a crowd.*

Vermont (vur-MONT): the fourteenth state of the United States.

The capital of VERMONT is Montpelier.

verve (vurv): a spirited and enthusiastic manner, particularly when embodied in an artistic performance; an air of vitality.

The critics were unanimous in their opinion that, although the plot of the play was implausible and its production values poor, the actress playing the librarian brought a unique VERVE to the role.

vex (vex): to irritate or bother.

Although his school friends constantly teased him about his ballet lessons, Ken never allowed their comments to VEX him.

viable (VIE-uh-bul): capable of being performed or occurring.

Mike argued quite persuasively that the only VIABLE solution to the company's financial dilemma was for it to go public and raise money by selling stock.

vial (VIE-ul): a small container (usually glass) used to hold liquids, medicines, and the like.

The doctor gave me a small VIAL of the drug for use over the weekend, and a written prescription so I could get more from the pharmacy on Monday.

viand (VIE-und): an article of food.

Chef Jacques thought that any VIAND, whether prime rib or meatloaf, should be served to the customer in a visually appealing way.

vicissitude (vih-SISS-ih-tude): a fateful obstacle or turn of events.

Aware that most of us are hurt by love's VICISSITUDES at some point during our lives, Max tried to forget the past and find someone new.

vilify (VIL-ih-fie): to defame; to slander.

My opponent's ceaseless attempts to VILIFY me during this campaign reached a new low when she accused me of being on the side of the neo-Nazi movement.

Virginia (vur-JIN-yuh): the tenth state of the United States.

The capital of VIRGINIA is Richmond.

virtually (VUR-choo-uh-lee): existing in effect, although not in actual fact or form.

Paul had been worried about his first day at work for weeks, so it came as a surprise to him when he passed his first day in the office with VIRTUALLY no nervousness.

virtuoso (vur-choo-OWE-so): a supremely skilled artist.

Geena is a piano VIRTUOSO who has won dozens of competitions.

viscosity (vis-KOSS-ih-tee): the thickness of a liquid.

The mechanic working on my car recommended I switch to a brand of motor oil with a higher VISCOSITY.

vivid (VIV-d): brilliant; resplendent and gaily colored. Also: described or capable of describing with great precision and detail; related in such a way as to leave a distinct impression.

Julius, a boy with a VIVID imagination, could amuse himself in his room for hours making up stories and adventures for his toy soldiers.

vivify (VIV-ih-fie): to bring to life; to make lively or active.

The characters in Keillor's stories are VIVIFIED through his almost uncanny sense of human nature and his knowledge of the importance of seemingly small events.

vociferous (vo-SIF-er-us): crying out loudly; noisy, especially in anger.

Anticipating a VOCIFEROUS reaction, I waited until we were well outside of the crowded restaurant before telling my father I had totaled the car.

volition (vo-LISH-un): the mental faculty associated with free will and unhindered, uncoerced choice.

Nothing you can say or do will be able to transform your father overnight; he will have to admit of his own VOLITION that he needs help and then make a commitment to work toward a recovery.

voluble (VOL-yuh-bul): talkative; gregarious.

Muriel's little girl is the most VOLUBLE two-year-old I've ever met; she rattled on endlessly until her mother sent her upstairs to play.

voluminous (vuh-LOO-mih-nuss): possessing great volume or fullness.

Michelle's wedding dress was so VOLUMINOUS that there was barely room for Jon to stand next to her at the altar.

259

vortex (VOR-tex): a whirlpool or whirlwind; a spinning mass of liquid or flame capable of drawing objects into it; something regarded as capable of drawing other entities into its current with great strength.

Even as the two nations slipped inexorably toward the VORTEX of war, the mainstream press focused on trivialities.

vouchsafe (vouch-SAFE): to deign or to condescend; to agree, in a condescending manner, to grant a request or do something; to offer as a favor or privilege.

James's show of superiority to everyone else in the family was so blatant that I'm surprised he VOUCHSAFED to spend a few minutes with me at the reunion.

vox populi (VOKS POP-yoo-lie): the voice of the people: public opinion.

I reject the idea that any ideologue who phones up a radio talk show represents the VOX POPULI.

wan (wahn): without color; pallid; pale.

Frankie looked thin and WAN after his long bout of mononucleosis.

wanderlust (WAN-dur-lust): a strong, innate desire to travel.

While Jerry told his family each Thanksgiving that he would someday settle down and raise a family, his irrepressible WANDERLUST kept him from putting down roots until he was well into his sixties.

wane (wane): to decrease in size, power, or intensity; to diminish; to decline.

Stanley took up French, dancing, backgammon—he even learned the basics of horticulture—anything to rekindle his girlfriend's WANING interest in their relationship.

wangle (WANG-gul): to get one's own way by using manipulation or clever means.

Franz WANGLED two tickets to the concert by pretending to be the son of the city's premier entertainment critic.

wary (WARE-ee): on guard; watchful of danger; leery; suspicious.

Although the new project has undeniable potential, I'm WARY about Ted's claim that he can bring the product to market by the first of January.

Washington (WASH-ing-ton): the forty-second state of the United States.

The capital of WASHINGTON is Olympia.

waver (WAY-vur): to sway; to quiver or flutter; also, to move back and forth on an issue before making a final decision.

Although the administration did its utmost to secure legislative support for the controversial initiative, three WAVERING senators announced their opposition to it last night, thus guaranteeing that the bill will never make its way out of committee.

West Virginia (west vur-JIN-yuh): the thirty-fifth state of the United States.

The capital of WEST VIRGINIA is Charleston.

whelp (hwelp): the offspring of a female dog or of certain other animals. Also, as a verb: to give birth to (used in connection with a female dog, wolf, lion, or similar animal).

Where is that little WHELP—he's taken my slipper again!

whet (hwet): to stimulate; also, to sharpen a knife or a similar object by honing on a stone.

Worried that I had eaten so little over the past few days, Mom tried to WHET my appetite by cooking my favorite foods: chicken fingers and mashed potatoes.

whey (whay): in cheesemaking, the liquid that separates from milk curd during coagulation.

Many parents, when asked by their children to identify exactly what Miss Muffet is eating in the famous nursery rhyme, are at a loss to explain "curds and WHEY."

whimsical (WIM-zih-kul): fanciful; given to acting on sudden notions or ideas.

John is known as a real sourpuss around the office, but as his college roommate I can tell you he has his WHIMSICAL side.

whippet (WIP-it): a short-haired, fast-running dog similar to a greyhound.

Like WHIPPETS straining before a race, the swimmers tensed at the edge of the pool, toes curled over the smooth stone of the starting line.

whittle (HWIT-ul): to shape a piece of wood and make it smooth by shaving or carving off pieces.

I thought WHITTLING was a pretty useless activity until I saw the beautiful walking stick Uncle Zeke had whittled for Grandpa.

who's (hooze): who is. (See, for comparison, the entry for *whose*.)

WHO'S going to the fair with me tonight?

whose (hooze): belonging to whom. (See, for comparison, the entry for *who's*.)

WHOSE idea was it to go to the fair tonight?

wile (wile): a clever trick meant to attain a goal; an instance of or talent for beguiling deceit. As a verb: to lure, entice, or beguile.

Headquarters trusts, as always, that the information with which you have been entrusted is secure even from the WILES of a spy of the opposite sex.

wily (WILE-ee): cunning; shrewd; clever or crafty.

Our WILY little puppy quickly learned that he could escape from the yard by digging a hole under the fence.

winsome (WIN-sum): pleasant; charming.

Although he had overslept and been in a terrific rush to get out of the house, a WINSOME glance from the vaguely familiar woman at the toll collection booth helped put Milton's morning back on track.

Wisconsin (wiss-KON-sin): the thirtieth state of the United States.

The capital of WISCONSIN is Madison.

wiseacre (WIZE-ake-ur): a know-it-all; one who professes to know everything.

"Listen, you little WISEACRE," Sergeant Artemis howled at Corporal Budworth, "if you think you can train these recruits better than I can, you ought to try it sometime."

withered (WITH-urd): shriveled; wrinkled and dried up.

It made Tim sad to realize that the oak tree he had such fun climbing as a child was now too WITHERED and old for his son to ascend safely.

witticism (WIT-ih-siz-um): a witty saying or remark.

We like to invite Roger to our cocktail parties, as he is able keep other guests entertained for hours on end with his stories and WITTICISMS.

wizened (WIZ-und): old; shriveled.

The subject of the documentary was a WIZENED old man of ninety-seven who happened to be the oldest living Bolshevik.

wok (wok): a bowl-shaped skillet used in Oriental cooking.

Jeb, who could work wonders in the kitchen with his WOK, treated us to an excellent stir-fried vegetable and chicken dish.

wont (wont): a habit or custom.

As was his WONT, Jeb took a walk to the sidewalk cafe near his home and bought a copy of the New York Times *to read.*

wrest (rest): to take away; to pull away forcefully.

When it comes to dealing with friends who are drunk and want to drive home by themselves, Mr. Powell advocates tactful suggestions, shrewd negotiation, and, if all else fails, an outright attempt to WREST the keys away from the person.

wunderkind (VOON-dur-kind): a child prodigy.

Although he died young, Mozart, a WUNDERKIND whose career in music began at the age of six, had a career that spanned two and half decades.

Wyoming (wye-OH-ming): the forty-fourth state of the United States.

The capital of WYOMING is Cheyenne.

xenophobe (ZEE-nuh-fobe): one who fears anything foreign or different; one who regards people, places, or customs that differ from one's own as inherently dangerous.

I don't believe my opponent is really a XENOPHOBE, despite his rhetoric against foreigners; he is simply a canny, wealthy, and extremely dangerous demagogue.

yabber (YAB-bur): to jabber; to chatter meaninglessly.

I am not interested in any of your YABBERING about how busy you've been at home; I want to know why this work is a month and a half late.

yammer (YAM-mer): to complain loudly; to whine.

While Diane was YAMMERING about how hard it was to get the office plants watered properly, I was trying to make a deadline.

yearling (YEER-ling): an animal that has entered its second year; also, a horse that is one year old, dating from the beginning of the year following its foaling.

Mr. Tompkin's prize YEARLING is a thoroughbred Clydesdale.

yeshiva (yuh-SHEE-vuh): a place of instruction in the Orthodox Jewish tradition for children of elementary school age.

When the YESHIVA released its children in the afternoon, the sounds of laughter echoed through the neighborhood.

yeti (YEH-tee): the (legendary) Abominable Snowman.

Carl claims to have photographic evidence of the Loch Ness Monster, several UFOs, and a large grey YETI, but I have yet to see any of it.

yippie (YIP-pee): a participant in a radical youth movement of the 1960s, the Youth International Party; one whose actions are reminiscent of the rebelliousness and irreverence of that time.

The YIPPIE protestors were on a collision course with Mayor Daley's riot police that night.

yob (yob): a hooligan or ruffian.

The first "YOB" may have been a tough customer from Liverpool, where the phrase originated.

yokel (YOE-kul): a bumpkin; a rustic person.

That one-set show may have impressed the YOKELS where you come from, but here in the big city we require a little more flash and stardust from our musicals.

yore (yore): former days; an era long past.

In days of YORE, scribes sat in their chambers copying out long manuscripts, and dreaming, I like to believe, of copiers and word processors.

your (yore): belonging to you. (See, for comparison, the entry for *you're*.)

> *Where is YOUR jacket, David?*

you're (yore): you are. (See, for comparison, the entry for *your*.)

> *Are you sure YOU'RE going to go to the party tonight?*

zephyr (ZEFF-ur): the west wind; any gentle wind.

> *Mike christened his new boat the ZEPHYR, even though he planned to use it primarily during the rugged winters of his native Massachusetts.*

zest (zest): gusto; vigor; spice; enjoyment.

> *Annabel's ZEST for life led her enthusiastically into modern dance, mountain climbing, and untold hours of volunteer work.*

zither (ZITH-ur): a small, harp-like stringed instrument.

> *An autoharp is similar to a ZITHER in that it has many strings and is strummed; because it has keys, however, the autoharp is easier to play.*

zymurgy (ZIE-mur-jee): the branch of chemistry concerned with fermentation.

> *Though not true chemists, brewers and winemakers could be considered lay experts in the field of ZYMURGY.*

Words You Should Know

by David Olsen, 235 pages, $6.95

1,200 essential words every educated person should be able to use and define.

Lots of people need a quick and authoritative way to identify and define the most troublesome common words. The original *Words You Should Know* features straightforward, succinct definitions and sentence examples for words that are tough but common. They're the kind of guides that can get you out of a jam, improve your performance at school, and help advance your career. And that's no hyperbole, rigmarole, or embellishment.

The Words You Should Know How to Spell

by Michelle Bevilacqua, 144 pages, $5.95

Indispensable. Commitment. Memento.
And yes, misspell.

Our language is often a perverse one. The words listed above seem simple enough, but they are just a few of the common English words that trip up writers— even the accomplished ones. Bevilacqua's newest book offers correct spelling and syllabification for these and 9,996 more entries, both *quotidian* and *weird*.

If you cannot find these titles at your favorite retail outlet, you may order them directly from the publisher. BY PHONE: Call 1-800-872-5627 (in Massachusetts 617-767-8100). We accept Visa, Mastercard, and American Express. $4.50 will be added to your total order for shipping and handling. BY MAIL: Write out the full title of the books you'd like to order and send payment, including $4.50 for shipping and handling, to: Adams Publishing, 260 Center Street, Holbrook, MA 02343. 30-day money-back guarantee.

A Note on Pronunciation

Pronunciation keys given in this book are rendered phonetically; no special symbols or systems have been employed.

Many of the words in this book have secondary and tertiary pronunciations—not listed here for the sake of simplicity—that are entirely correct. Furthermore, regional influences often affect the pronunciations of certain words. What has been offered is the most common accepted means of pronouncing a given word, but not necessarily the only way.